THE EASY WAY TO ENJOY FLYING

The common thread running through Allen Carr's work is the removal of fear. Indeed, his genius lies in eliminating the phobias and anxieties which prevent people from being able to enjoy life to the full, as his bestselling books *Allen Carr's Easy Way to Stop Smoking, The Only Way to Stop Smoking Permanently, Allen Carr's Easyweigh to Lose Weight, How to Stop Your Child Smoking,* and now *The Easy Way to Enjoy Flying,* vividly demonstrate.

A successful accountant, Allen Carr's hundred-cigarettes-a-day addiction was driving him to despair until, in 1983, after countless failed attempts to quit, he finally discovered what the world had been waiting for – the Easy Way to Stop Smoking. He has now built a network of clinics that span the globe and has a phenomenal reputation for success in helping smokers to quit. His books have been published in over twenty languages and video, audio and CD-ROM versions of his method are also available.

Tens of thousands of people have attended Allen Carr's clinics where, with a success rate of over 90 per cent, he guarantees that you will find it easy to quit smoking or your money back. A full list of clinics appears in the back of this book. Should you require any assistance do not hesitate to contact your nearest therapist. Weight control sessions are now offered at a selection of these clinics. A full corporate service is also available enabling companies to implement no-smoking policies simply and effectively. All correspondence and enquiries about ALLEN CARR'S BOOKS, VIDEOS, AUDIO TAPES AND CD-ROMS should be addressed to the London Clinic.

The Easyway to Enjoy Flying

Allen Carr

ARCTURUS

Published by
Arcturus Publishing Limited

This edition published 2000

Printed and bound by Omnia Books Ltd in the UK

ISBN: 1-55267-130-5

To Adelle Mirer, who made me aware of the millions for whom the pleasure of flying is a nightmare

CONTENTS

INTRODUCTION

I was a 60-a-day confirmed smoker for over 20 years. Like most heavy smokers I'd made several attempts to quit. In the early days I tried willpower. It didn't take long to discover that I had none. On later attempts I tried acupuncture, hypnosis, nicotine gum and patches. They all seemed to work for a limited period. It wasn't that I was climbing the wall, but I could never lose that feeling of being a smoker who was no longer allowed to smoke. Like most ex-smokers, at certain times the craving for a cigarette became irresistible and I was soon back on 60 a day.

I'd heard about Allen Carr. I'd seen him on television and I even knew a couple of people who had successfully stopped after attending one of his clinics. In fact my husband had bought me one of his books. I feel stupid now that I didn't bother to read it there and then, but I'm very sceptical; I already knew that smoking was killing me and costing me a fortune. Stopping wasn't my problem. I could stop smoking but I couldn't see how a book could remove that feeling of losing a crutch and a friend.

Some three years later, while searching for some other object, I came across the book again. I'd already given up even trying to give up, so why I started to read it, I do not know. I was riveted. I wasn't reading about Allen Carr's experiences but my own autobiography. When I completed the book I smoked my final cigarette and I have never had the slightest desire to smoke another.

Apart from smoking, there were two other areas in my life that caused me considerable aggravation. Ironically, one of them was that since my early twenties I'd had a permanent fight with the flab. Since the majority of middle-aged, married women with two children have the same problem, why should this be ironic? Because I'd always maintained that my reason for starting to smoke in the first place, and for continuing to smoke, was to reduce weight.

By now Allen Carr was my guru. However, when I heard that he had applied his method to weight reduction and that it was just as easy and enjoyable to be the exact weight that you want to be as it is to stop smoking, I was again sceptical. After all, as Allen himself says:

> Smoking is foul, poisonous and a killer, whereas eating is pleasurable, marvellous and a life-saver.

I'm ashamed that I doubted him. He is absolutely right. You may have already deduced that my third problem was a manic fear of flying. Allen fully explains the lies and self-deceit that smokers, alcoholics and other drug addicts are forced to resort to. I've no need to explain to fellow sufferers that these are minimal compared to those afflicted with a fear of flying. I've no intention of elaborating on the panic I used to go through at the mere thought of having to fly, and the intricate web of lies I would weave in order to avoid doing so, because these matters are fully discussed in the text. I now realize that those lies not only didn't fool me but didn't fool my family and friends either. They were just too polite and compassionate to make me feel aware, not only of the loss of pleasure that my fear of flying caused me, but also of the loss of pleasure that they suffered.

When Allen told me that he had also once suffered the same panic at the thought of flying and that he now looked upon flying, not as some frightening ordeal that has to be first undergone in order to enjoy a holiday abroad, but as an interesting, enjoyable and exciting part of that holiday or business trip, I asked him what had made the difference. By now my faith in Allen was such that I had no reason to be sceptical. However, I was. After all, smoking and over-eating are things that people do but wish they didn't. Flying is the complete opposite, it's something that people would love to enjoy but can't.

We spent two hours talking to each other. Bear in mind that, up to that time, not only had I never flown, but I had never had the courage even to visit an airport or to contemplate booking a flight. When we finished our chat I had tears in my eyes. I emphasize they were tears of joy. I couldn't wait to book a holiday abroad, not because I needed a holiday, but because by the end of that chat I'd already lost my fear of flying and couldn't wait to prove it.

Adelle Mirer

1   Who wants to go abroad anyway?

It was the time when holidays to the sunspots – Majorca, the Canaries, Tenerife and, if you were doing really well, to Florida and the Bahamas – were not exactly commonplace, but becoming relatively inexpensive and fashionable.

I was a recently qualified accountant. My income, car and house were slightly better than the average of my friends and my mortgage was slightly lower. However, while I still regarded two weeks in an up-market holiday camp at Bognor Regis as the holiday of a lifetime, my friends were luxuriating in the sunshine of the Mediterranean.

Why didn't I follow the fashion? Was it because I was loyal to the British holiday industry? No. Was it because the weather at Bognor is so superior to the Mediterranean? No need to answer that one. Perhaps it was because I really enjoyed two weeks in a holiday camp? I hope I don't sound snobbish, but the answer is no. Was it the food? I've no doubt the food was as enjoyable and nutritious as anything available at the exotic holiday resorts, but my main relief at the end of the holiday was to enjoy home cooking again. The obvious answer is that it was the cost: two weeks at a holiday camp at Bognor would be much cheaper than two weeks on the Mediterranean. Amazingly it was the complete reverse. Eventually, when I did pluck up enough courage to take that first flight (forgive me, I'm still kidding myself: when I was first forced into that first horrendous flight), we got two weeks in Majorca, including the return flight and full board at a 4-star hotel for £32 per adult and half price for children.

I'm aware that I must sound like a Monty Python character saying: "I can remember when you could hire a coach and four to Romano's, enjoy a ballet at Covent Garden followed by supper at the Ritz and still have change from half-a-crown." The fact is that the equivalent holiday at Bognor would have cost me more than double the trip to Majorca and this is probably why the travel company eventually went broke. However, that was their problem and not mine. The true reason I hadn't seriously considered a holiday abroad was that I'd never been in an airplane and I was apprehensive about flying, though at that time, I was not consciously aware of the fact. Over 30 years later, it is difficult for me to remember my exact feelings and I'm well aware of the ability of alcoholics, nicotine and other drug addicts to deceive themselves.

I'm assuming that anyone who has taken the trouble to read this book will have more than just an apprehension about flying and will regard panic as a more suitable description. However, at the time I can say with certainty that apprehension rather than fear described my true feelings. After all, I'd chosen to serve my national service in the RAF rather than the army or navy, although the only RAF airplane that I saw throughout my two years' service was a stationary Spitfire at the entrance to the reception station at Padgate. But I did apply to be trained as a pilot. Needless to say, I was not accepted. The point is that I would not have applied if I'd had a genuine fear of flying at that time.

Back to the holiday. It was the suggestion of another couple, and as the Godfather would have put it: £32 for two weeks, including flight and full board? It was an offer we couldn't refuse. We met several times prior to the holiday. They were evenings of intense excitement as we planned and anticipated the marvellous time we'd all have. This is a practice that I thoroughly recommend. The most carefully planned holiday can end up a complete disaster, but the exhilaration of the anticipation of it (the marvellous holiday not the disaster!) can be enjoyed many times before the actual event.

FROM APPREHENSION TO PARANOIA

2   From apprehension to paranoia

It was not only the first time that any of us had flown, including our children, but the first time we'd had an exotic holiday abroad. However, for me, far from being exciting, those meetings became sheer hell. Long before the departure the apprehension rapidly developed through genuine fear to out-and-out paranoia. I knew why I was frightened. Although I knew that, statistically, flying was the safest form of transport, I was obsessed with thoughts about all the things that could go wrong. There seemed to be so many and, at 35,000 feet, it only needed one of them.

During the weeks leading up to the flight, I couldn't concentrate during the day and lay awake half the night, imagining all the things that could go wrong. Ironically, my greatest fear was that I wouldn't have the courage to go through with it. The actual flight was a living nightmare. Some of the details are now vague, but my feeling of panic was not alleviated by an eight-hour delay culminating in a mad scramble across the tarmac, dragging a child with one arm and carrying a three-year-old under the other.

I don't normally suffer from claustrophobia, but the plane looked minute. If I was hoping that the effect would be similar to Dr Who's telephone box, such hopes were soon dashed. The interior seemed microscopic and when the exit door was closed, it was as if a giant hand had crushed my windpipe. I white-knuckled my way throughout the flight.

It soon became obvious that the runway wasn't long enough to complete the take-off. It was all my fault. If only I hadn't insisted on taking my golf clubs. Obviously it was that extra weight that was causing the problem. I interpreted every grunt and groan in the hydraulic system, every change in the pitch of the engines, every variation in height or direction, as impending disaster. Even the rather pleasant chime of the PA system became the inevitable harbinger of doom. "PING" – Oh dear God, the captain is going to announce that we are about to crash-land in the sea. Those panic seconds that seem like hours before we realize that all they are really informing us of is that we can now smoke, or undo our seat-belts, or that drinks, meals or duty-frees are now being served.

When we finally touched down safely, and as the plane rapidly decelerated from the speed that I estimated to be about 500 mph to 60 mph, I remember the intense feeling of relief. I thought: "Even if something does go wrong now, at least we'll survive." When the plane finally came to rest, there was a moment of utter joy. We'd made it safely. At least I could enjoy two weeks in the sun before the return flight. The joy ended with the realization of the last three words. Before I even got off the plane, I started to worry about the return flight and the whole two weeks was obsessed with and ruined by the thought.

I feel that society generally is far too flippant about people who suffer from a fear of flying, which from now on I will refer to as FOF. We grind our guts out throughout the year to earn the reward of a couple of weeks in some exotic location. A sizeable proportion of our annual earnings is put aside to pay for the cost. Through no fault of our own, we happen to suffer from FOF. Instead of being a reward, our annual holiday becomes a nightmare and it doesn't just last for two weeks. It starts the moment we commit ourselves to the flight and doesn't end until the return journey is safely completed. Even then the problem hasn't been solved: you know you have to go through the same misery for the rest of your life.

I PROMISE YOU THAT YOU DON'T!!!

Not only that you don't, but that, provided you follow all the instructions, by the time you have finished this book, you'll be just like Adelle: straining at the leash and looking forward to your next flight even if it happens to be your first flight. Your first instruction is:

TO FOLLOW ALL THE INSTRUCTIONS

Every instruction I give you is important. The first is the most important because, provided you follow it, you cannot fail.

The next two instructions are the only difficult ones that I will ask you to follow. Your second instruction is to:

KEEP AN OPEN MIND

Now, we all like to feel that we are open-minded and you might have complacently flipped past this instruction without a second thought. If so, you have already failed to follow it. I need you to be sceptical of and to question not only everything I say to you, but everything you've heard from the rest of society no matter from what source. In particular, I need you to question your own views, even to the extent of not deciding whether you actually have a fear of flying until you've finished the book.

You are probably apprehensive at this stage. This might be due to fear of failure or the fear that I'll persuade you to take a flight which will turn out to be a disaster. I do not mean that the plane will crash but that the flight will be a terrible trauma for you.

You might not realize it at this time, but fear of flying is purely a mental problem and, as such, can be overcome by anyone. Airports are exciting and fascinating places and flying can be equally exhilarating, providing you don't suffer from FOF. If you do suffer from FOF, they are anathema. You are in the happy situation of having so much to gain and absolutely nothing to lose. The worst thing that can happen to you is that I fail to help to remove your fear of flying, in which case, you'll be no worse off than when you started.

If you start off with a feeling of doom and gloom, you won't necessarily guarantee failure but you will be making it much more likely and in all probability will have to re-read the book one or more times.

So your third instruction is to:

START OFF IN A HAPPY FRAME OF MIND

Now we have a chicken-and-egg situation here. If I could first convince you that the book will enable anyone and everyone who suffers from FOF, including you, to lose that fear, you would already be in that frame of mind. However, if you start with a feeling of gloom and doom, you are more likely to finish with one. I need you to trust me. After all, I won't ask you to use willpower. I won't even ask you to use courage. All I'm asking you to do is to read this book with an open mind. Nothing bad is happening. On the contrary, something marvellous is happening. See it as an exciting challenge. Take pride and pleasure in overcoming your fear. Also give me the pleasure of helping you to do so.

When I ask you to trust me, I'm not asking you to have faith in me. During the book I will explain everything to you. By the end of the book you will have no need to have faith in me and by then you will trust me. Perhaps it will enable you to start off in the right frame of mind if I explain more about:

MY METHOD

3   My method

You will have deduced from Adelle's introduction that my initial claim to fame was that I discovered a method that would enable any smoker to find it easy to quit immediately and permanently, without suffering withdrawal pangs or using willpower, gimmicks or substitutes.

Smokers arrive at my clinic in various states of panic and leave four hours later already happy non-smokers. After two years my reputation was such that smokers would fly from all over the world to attend my clinics and it soon became a losing battle, trying to find time to assist them all.

So I incorporated my method into a book: *The Easy Way to Stop Smoking.* "EASYWAY" has been a best-seller for all of the 14 years since its initial publication by Penguin and is now translated into over twenty languages. As I write, it is a best-seller in Holland and the No. 1 best-seller (non-fiction) in Germany.

At the time, I felt that my discovery related purely to smoking. During the thousands of group sessions that I subsequently conducted, it gradually began to dawn on me that my method would be just as effective for any drug addiction, including alcohol and heroin, or indeed, any problem or phobia that is purely mental. Perhaps you believe that problems like nicotine, heroin and alcohol, because they are all poisons, are mainly physical problems. Not so. They are only problems because we take them. Arsenic and strychnine are also powerful poisons; however, they present no problem to us because we have no need or desire to take them.

It is the belief that we obtain some pleasure or crutch from nicotine, heroin or alcohol that is the true cause of the problem. Even if you believe that the problem is physical or partially physical, the solution is purely mental. Remove the need or desire to take the poison and the problem is solved.

Adelle visualized quitting smoking and removing a fear of flying as complete opposites. So how can the same method solve both problems? I have to admit that at first her view appeared to be logical. Smoking could accurately be described as:

> A pastime in which the one-in-two risk of death doesn't prevent smokers from participating.

Whereas flying could be described with equal accuracy as:

> A pastime in which certain people would dearly love to participate but the less than one-in-several-millions risk of death prevents them from doing so.

Ironically there are literally millions of people on the planet that suffer from both problems. The famous golfer Neil Coles was a classic example. His fear of flying prevented him from earning millions of dollars on the American circuit, yet he would chain-smoke round the golf course.

Stopping smoking and removing a fear of flying might on the surface appear to be complete opposites. Someone who has suffered FOF, like myself, might deduce: persuading someone to quit smoking is trying to convince them to stop doing something they enjoy doing because it's dangerous. Whereas persuading someone to overcome their fear of flying is like persuading someone to do what they hate doing because it isn't dangerous.

Am I removing the confusion? Of course not. On the contrary, all I'm doing is adding to it. It is the confusion that causes the problem. Let's consider the two problems again. Smokers will wax lyrical, elaborating on the delights of being a smoker. They'll tell you how marvellous cigarettes taste – it doesn't seem to occur to them that they don't eat them. They'll tell you how smoking helps to relieve boredom and stress and how it assists concentration and relaxation – it doesn't seem to occur to them that boredom and concentration are complete opposites, as are stressful and relaxing occasions, or how the identical cigarette out of the same packet can have the complete opposite effect to the previous one.

In spite of all these marvellous advantages that smokers firmly believe that cigarettes possess, ask any smoker if they encourage their children to smoke and you'll be left in no doubt that every smoker on the planet hates the thought of their children becoming hooked. Ask smokers why they don't encourage their children to enjoy the pleasures or crutch that smoking provides and they will waffle and flounder.

Isn't the real problem with smokers that the rational part of their brains is telling them that they shouldn't smoke, and at the same time the irrational part is trying to convince them that they should? They know this is true and that's why they hate the thought of their children becoming hooked.

Isn't the real problem with people who have a fear of flying that their rational brain is saying it's perfectly safe to fly, and their irrational brain is saying no it isn't?

In both cases the problem is the same: it's schizophrenia. We are at one and the same time two different people. Part of our brain says smoke – another part says don't. Part of our brain says fly – another part says flying is dangerous.

Perhaps you feel that it is the rational part of your brain that says don't fly and the irrational part that says fly. Either way it doesn't matter. It is only the schizophrenia and the confusion, that cause the problem. There are many people on this planet that have never flown who do not suffer from the schizophrenia. They are quite happy not to fly and many of them are highly intelligent people.

From what I have just said, you might well conclude that your solution is to join their ranks. It would be indeed unfortunate if you did, for those people, while content with their lot, are not aware of what they are missing. So what! Ignorance is bliss. Yes, but it only remains bliss while you remain ignorant. I once reached the stage with smoking where I gave up even trying to quit. My attitude was: I'd rather have the shorter and, as I believed at the time, sweeter life of being a smoker. I argued that the misery of being a smoker outweighed the misery of life without cigarettes. I'm so grateful that I did quit and that life is so much more enjoyable in so many ways as a non-smoker. My only regret is that I didn't discover the secret of making it easy to quit earlier in my life.

The world is your oyster. I don't know who first coined that expression or how old it is, but whoever and whenever, it can never have been more true than it is today. Can you envy someone who has never learned to drive? Isn't it similar to not being able to walk? Isn't not being able to fly, or finding it traumatic if you pluck up enough courage to do so, equally debilitating? Today, flying is relatively cheap and no longer the exclusive pleasure of the rich. Now the world is our oyster. The beautiful truth is that flying is a wonderful and exhilarating experience, that it is safe and that a fear of flying is irrational.

I've asked you to open your mind and to start off with a feeling of exhilaration. I'm not asking you to use psychology: the pessimist sees the bottle as half empty and the optimist sees it as half full. With flying, the bottle is actually full but someone who suffers from FOF perceives it as empty.

Let's take a closer look at:

THE CONFUSION AND THE BRAINWASHING

4   The confusion and the brainwashing

Shortly after I had discovered my method I was approached by the doctor who at that time was considered to be the leading expert in the UK on helping smokers to quit. The broadcaster Derek Jameson had successfully used my method to quit and invited me to appear on his BBC program. The doctor heard the broadcast, told me how impressed he was and invited me to attend his clinic.

Initially I was flattered, but later piqued, when he explained that he had invited me, not to pick my brains, but so that I could pick up some pointers from him. He explained how he had categorized smokers into nine different types and how he and his colleagues were working on producing a non-addictive cigarette. My pique was quickly replaced by sympathy when it dawned on me that he'd spent his whole life searching for the solution and even failed to recognize it when it was plainly pointed out to him.

There are many different types of smoker. There are heavy smokers, casual smokers, young smokers, old smokers, smokers that smoke to relieve boredom or stress, social smokers or smokers who smoke because they believe it helps them to relax or concentrate. There are habitual smokers and addictive smokers. There are smokers who prefer cigarettes, roll-ups, cigars or pipes. The doctors and psychologists spent many hours trying to analyse the myriad types and trying to persuade them not to smoke.

I was lucky. I discovered that there was only one type of smoker – the type who believed that he or she got some sort of pleasure or crutch from smoking. At the same time I realized that the crutch or pleasure was just a subtle illusion.

Why was my method so successful? Because it was the complete opposite to other methods. Other methods would concentrate on the tremendous disadvantages of being a smoker: the risk of contracting horrendous diseases, the waste of money, the filth, the stigma, the slavery. In other words, they concentrated on the stupidities of being a smoker. It never seemed to occur to them that smokers were more aware than they were of the stupidity of being a smoker, that smokers do not smoke for the reasons that they shouldn't and that the real problem is to remove the reasons that compel them to continue to smoke.

What was the great discovery that I had made to enable any smoker to find it easy to quit immediately and permanently? It was simply this:

I REMOVED THE CONFUSION

The terrible torture that smokers suffer when they try to quit isn't the terrible withdrawal pains from nicotine, but the belief that they are making a genuine sacrifice, that they get some genuine pleasure or crutch from smoking and that, deprived of their little crutch or friend, they'll neither be able to fully enjoy social occasions nor be equipped to handle stress. They also believe that they would have to endure some awful trauma in order to be free and that they would need courage, willpower and discipline in order to do so.

I first explained the mysteries of the nicotine trap: why smokers are perfectly capable of enjoying social occasions and coping with stress before they become hooked on nicotine, and how smoking, far from relieving boredom or stress, or aiding concentration or relaxation, actually does the complete opposite. I would also explain why, once they had extinguished the final cigarette, they would enjoy social occasions more, be better equipped to handle stress and, most important of all, why they wouldn't spend the rest of their lives moping for a cigarette.

The important thing was that I removed the confusion and fear before they extinguished their final cigarette. When they did so, they were already non-smokers and could enjoy being non-smokers immediately, knowing that they were already better equipped to handle stress and that they would enjoy social occasions more.

How will my method help to remove your fear of flying? The key lies in Adelle's introduction. She describes her surprise that after our chat she was transformed from a person with what she regarded as a paranoid fear of flying to someone who was actually looking forward to the experience. At the time, I was both aware of and very pleased with her reaction. However, I confess that my surprise at her reaction was many times greater than hers. I had no intention of trying to remove her problem; on the contrary, we were merely having an informal chat during which I confessed my former terror of flying.

At the time, although I no longer had the terror, I had never lost my apprehension about flying, yet Adelle had clearly lost hers and it was equally obvious that it was a direct result of our chat. When I was invited to write a book about FOF, I was non-committal. After all, I didn't fully understand why I was still apprehensive and yet Adelle no longer had a problem. Ironically, it wasn't until I started to conduct the necessary research for the book that I fully understood why Adelle had completely lost her fear and why that research enabled me to lose any remaining apprehension that I had retained about flying.

Part of that research was to read books and listen to audio tapes by other experts. It soon became apparent that the advice, as well-meaning as it might be, was usually not so much to remove the fear of flying, as to develop techniques to enable sufferers to cope with their fears and fly in spite of them. Like so much of modern medicine, whether it be the cure of physical or mental disease, the principal object appeared to be to remove the symptoms of the disease rather than the cause.

I'm referring to panic and anxiety attacks, pounding heart, difficulty in breathing, sweaty palms and any other unpleasant physical effects that people who have a fear of flying tend to suffer from. The unpleasant physical effects themselves, together with the fear that you might suffer from them, are the direct result of your fear of flying. We are going to remove your fear of flying, which will automatically remove any unpleasant physical effects that you might have suffered. It will also remove the fear that you might suffer them. To advise techniques to cope with these physical effects is effectively saying: your fear of flying is the result of the unpleasant physical effects – learn to cope with those and you will gradually conquer your fear of flying.

All this does is to increase the confusion that already exists. I should also make it clear that my method is not a gradual process of learning to live and cope with the fear. I was a schoolboy boxing champion who had a fear of spiders. The same culture that had convinced me that there was something heroic about trying to bash out the brains of some other unfortunate youth, while you desperately tried to protect your own, had taught me to be ashamed of my fear of spiders – men aren't afraid of spiders – only girls can afford this privilege. I decided to cure my fear.

I'd find a tiny spider and hold it in my closed hand. I'd repeat the exercise with increasingly larger spiders until I progressed to the stage when I held a great hairy monster in my hand. At this stage the thought would occur to me: "What am I doing – I HATE SPIDERS!"

To this day I still hate spiders. Trying to face up to the problem didn't cure it. However, I've learned to live with it. Many other people admit to being frightened of spiders, and I've long suspected that many of those that deny it are being somewhat untruthful. Why else would they need to hold a huge, hairy monster in their hands? I'm not afraid of lumps of sugar, but I don't find it necessary to hold one for several seconds in order to prove the fact. If there's a spider on the ceiling, I won't walk directly beneath it. If it's on the floor, I will without conscience step on it.

I'm told that my fear of spiders is a phobia and irrational because there are no spiders in the UK that can cause me any harm. I'm aware of that fact. Someone spitting on the pavement or dog's excrement doesn't harm me either, but both cause me offence so I do my best to avoid them. If dog turds possessed the same unfortunate characteristics that spiders do, of having eight legs that pop out from secluded places when you least expect them, of being able to drop on you from the ceiling at the speed of sound yet remain silent, and spin invisible clinging webs the exact height of your face so that you don't even know whether the spider is in it when you walk into it, then I'd be frightened of dog turds even though they still wouldn't harm me. I do not regard my attitude to spiders as a phobia – it has always been the same and always will be.

Perhaps you feel the same about your attitude to flying? There are two important differences:

1 Even if my fear of spiders is irrational, I'm quite happy to go through life avoiding them, I don't have this awful feeling that I'm missing out.

2 A fear of flying is irrational. It is caused by a misapprehension that flying is unsafe or unpleasant. Remove that misapprehension and you remove the fear.

Now I can hear you shouting:

I KNOW FLYING IS SAFE BUT I STILL HAVE
THE FEAR!!!

No, you don't *know* that flying is safe. You may have been bombarded with statistics proving that flying is the safest form of travel. Your rational mind might even believe those statistics. But at the same time, from birth you have also been bombarded and brainwashed with information which tells you that flying is unnatural and dangerous.

It's the schizophrenia, the confusion, that causes the problem. We are going to remove this confusion. The first step is to take a look at:

THE BIG Q

5   The big Q

What is the big Q? It is a questionnaire that I requested hundreds of sufferers of FOF to complete. I just couldn't believe many of the facts and theories that I had read in the books written by the experts, and needed to check out their credibility.

I was hoping that the big Q would help to remove much of the confusion. Eventually it did but initially it merely added to it. As I personally loathe completing forms and questionnaires, I designed it so that the majority of the questions needed a simple yes or no answer. Over 300 sufferers completed the form. The results are shown in Appendix A.

I had expected the answers to conform to the experience that I suffered, described in the opening chapters. I felt my fears were irrational and cowardly and I was ashamed of myself. Yet many sufferers of FOF describe the complete opposite emotions. With the knowledge I had then, my fear was perfectly rational. Far from being cowardly I was in fact being very brave. Why? Because in spite of believing that I was risking my life, I got on that plane and never told a soul about the misery I went through. At the same time I felt very stupid. Why? Because I was ashamed of myself but kept it to myself. My fear of dying was actually superseded by my fear of losing face in the eyes of my wife, children and friends. After all, just like my fear of spiders, society had conditioned me to believe that men didn't suffer from fear, fear was the exclusive privilege of women and children.

Years later I learned that all four of us had the same apprehensions. Yet each of us stupidly kept it to ourselves. I can't believe that the other three went through the same nightmare that I suffered prior to, during and after that holiday, but I do know that it would have been more pleasurable, or the ordeal less miserable, had we had the courage to declare and share our misgivings. I truly believe that my apprehension would not have degenerated into a nightmare had I known that I wasn't alone.

It might be that in spite of your fear of flying you've had the courage to endure the ordeal on one or more occasions as I did. If so you have every reason to be proud of yourself. Conversely, perhaps your fear is such that you've booked flights, but cancelled at the eleventh hour, or you've actually boarded the plane and got off before take-off and never had the courage to fly. Does this mean that you are less courageous than I and have reason to be ashamed of yourself? Or does it mean that you are less stupid than I was? How at one and the same time could I have felt both brave and stupid?

These apparently conflicting emotions can be very confusing, particularly when we are young. Perhaps another episode in my youth will help to remove the confusion. I refer to:

MY EXPERIENCE WITH EUGINE

6   My experience with Eugine

It happened when I was a young audit clerk, and I'm afraid that I'm back on my Monty Python theme. At the time, I was struggling to survive on a salary of £2 per week. Although we were paid like paupers, we were expected to conduct ourselves like lords. Accordingly, we were entitled to claim travelling expenses on the basis of the first-class rail fare from our City office to the client's premises. Needless to say, we all travelled third class.

On this particular occasion the client was situated in Biggleswade. I do not wish to cause offence to residents of Biggleswade but, in those days at least, it was a one-horse town. Altogether four starving clerks had been allocated to this audit and one of them, whom I shall refer to as Eugine, had the bright idea of hiring a car.

In those days, only the very rich actually owned a car. I complimented him and thought what an excellent accountant he would make. Not only would we all profit from the difference between the first- and third-class fares, but we could each save approximately 2 shillings on the third-class rail fare.

I was very naive then. It never occurred to me that this lad had no more desire to be an accountant than I had. He was a motor-racing fanatic. His true motive was not to save a few shillings, but to satisfy his fantasies of being Stirling Moss at Le Mans, by hurtling up the A1 at 80 mph in a clapped-out Austin A40.

Now, I'm aware that 80 mph will not impress the modern driver. However, in those days motorists regarded 40 mph as hurtling, whereas today it might be regarded as driving dangerously slowly. It was also pre-seat-belts. Not only was it commonplace to drive on bald tires, but you were regarded as somewhat extravagant if you replaced them before they burst and, at that time, long stretches of the A1 did not have medians.

Have you noticed how we all seem to have a predilection to do the one thing that physically and mentally we are least equipped to do? How 280-pound, middle-aged ladies like to wear cat suits and leotards? I've heard that Pavarotti's real ambition was to be a ballet dancer.

Eugine was exceedingly short-sighted. I don't mean that he couldn't forecast events, but that he hadn't got 20/20 vision. I've no doubt that with the incredible technological advances in modern lenses, his deficient eyesight would not have been apparent. But in those days his were called bottle glasses. The lenses were almost an inch thick, they grossly distorted the wearer's eyes and it was impossible not to notice them.

I don't think it would have been so bad if one had formed the impression that his spectacles in some way compensated for his bad eyesight. However, his habit of leaning forward with his nose almost touching the windscreen as he was driving, gave the impression that he couldn't see properly.

I considered myself fortunate that I was in a rear passenger seat. It didn't seem to bother him that he leaned so far forward that he couldn't see into the rear-view mirror. Perhaps I'm maligning him unjustly. In those days, at the speed he was travelling, there was little point in glancing at the rear-view mirror. To make matters worse, he had this annoying habit that many drivers have of taking his eyes off the road whenever he spoke to anyone. I know it's polite to look at people when you talk to them but when you're driving a car it's also very dangerous. Every time he did it I was tempted to grab his ears and straighten his head. I sat terrified in complete silence throughout the journey from London to Biggleswade and the return to London.

During the weekend I explained to my wife that I thought Eugine was a dangerous driver and that, I would rather travel by train the following week. The trouble was that, if I did that, the car hire would no longer be profitable. I spent a very unpleasant weekend. If I opted out I would have to give a valid reason. I could either have admitted that I was terrified, which would have made me feel cowardly and lose face, or I could have denigrated Eugine's driving, which would have made me feel even more cowardly because, at that time in my life, with my confused thinking, I would have believed that the only reason that I had criticized his driving was to disguise my irrational fear.

I was quite proud of myself that I was brave enough to overcome my fear and go through the same nightmare the second week and, had Eugine not overturned the car doing 80 mph the third week, I would still be proud of myself to this day.

Have you heard of the expression:

CONSCIENCE MAKES COWARDS OF US ALL

I'd often used that expression during my life without even considering what it meant. It's amazing how we are able to do this: Look before you leap -- He who hesitates is lost. They are complete contradictions, yet we will use them to justify our actions if it suits us.

I said I was proud that I was brave enough to overcome my fear and I was. At the same time I still felt cowardly that I hadn't had the guts to back my true judgement by taking the train. The accident proved to me that I had made the wrong decision. How ridiculous that I was prepared to risk my very life to save 2 shillings. It took less courage to face the nightmare again than it did to admit my fear and at the same time risk embarrassing and offending my colleague. I felt cowardly, but was it because I didn't want to admit to my fear, or was it because I had a conscience about embarrassing my friend? Who knows? All I can tell you is that in a similar incident years later, on what was meant to be a relaxed weekend in Paris, I had no compunction or hesitation in telling the driver, who was the 50-year-old equivalent to Eugine: "I'm sitting here terrified and unless you slow down or let me drive, I'd be obliged if you would pull over and let me out."

I felt no embarrassment about my own fear because I knew that he was driving recklessly. I admit that I did suffer some apprehension in case I had embarrassed him. Even on that score I needn't have worried. Far from taking offence, he apologized and reduced his speed so that the journey became a pleasure rather than a nightmare. On that occasion there was no conflict in my mind. I believe that conscience can make us appear to be cowards. However, I think a more apt expression would be, not conscience makes cowards of us all but:

CONFUSION MAKES COWARDS OF US ALL

In the earlier example my mind was confused. I risked my life rather than embarrass a friend. That was crass stupidity. Fortunately I had learned my lesson by the time of the later incident. There was no confusion.

Now, you might well be wondering what all this has to do with overcoming your fear of flying. In fact you could be excused for concluding that the message that I'm trying to convey is that if you believe flying is dangerous, you should have the courage to accept that fact and refuse to do it. If flying were dangerous, I would support you 100 per cent.

No, I'm merely trying to remove the confusion. People who suffer from FOF fall into two basic categories:

1 Those who in spite of their fear have had the courage actually to fly.

2 Those who have never plucked up sufficient courage to overcome their fear and consequently have never flown.

The distinction is a fallacy. If I fall within category 1, I can say to you: "At least I've had the courage to face my fear." You as a category-2 non-flyer can riposte: "What do you know about the fear of flying? If you suffered a mere tenth of the traumas that I do, you wouldn't go within ten miles of an airport."

This is the truly terrible part of any illness or affliction, be it mental or physical: it is so lonely: it is only you that can appreciate your suffering. It's true that two people can suffer from FOF or any other disease and that they might be of some comfort to each other by discussing the problem. However, it is my experience that they may cause more problems than they cure if such discussions are allowed to degenerate into a competition about who suffers more, and if they involve exchanging misleading and destructive information.

In case you are left wondering about the devastation that followed Eugine's overturning of the car at 80 mph, I'm happy to inform you that, by some miracle, the worst any of the four occupants suffered were mild scratches and bruises. I'm even more happy to tell you that I was lucky enough to escape without even those. However, I'm convinced that the experience did later contribute to my fear of flying.

As I will emphasize throughout, it is the schizophrenia, the confusion, that causes the problem: am I a fool and a coward because I know that flying is safe yet cannot pluck up enough courage to do it? Or, if I can pluck up enough courage, am I stupid for risking my life and subjecting myself to the trauma?

Let's take a closer look at the real cause of the problem:

FEAR

7 Fear

Whether you believe that we are the creation of a god or some equally powerful intelligence, whether you believe that we are the pinnacle of 3 billion years of natural selection, or whether you believe, as I do, that evolution and natural selection are merely the processes that whatever intelligence has created us uses to achieve perfection, only a fool would dispute that a healthy human body controlled by a healthy human brain is the most powerful creature on this planet.

We are equipped with several guiding forces to ensure that we survive, whether we like it or not. One of those guiding forces is fear. Many people think of fear as a form of weakness or cowardice. But without a fear of fire, of heights, of drowning, of being attacked, we would not survive.

At our stop-smoking clinics I cannot count the number of times I have heard smokers say: "I suffer with my nerves." As if feeling nervous were some form of disease. The door slams. You jump 2 feet in the air. That isn't bad nerves. It is good nerves. Watch starlings feeding, they appear oblivious to what's happening around them, but the slightest sound will cause them to fly off as one. That sound signified "CAT" and it's the bird that doesn't jump who gets eaten by the cat.

We think of fear as an evil. We admire people who are fearless. We've got it all back to front. Fear is our protection. It is a warning sign. It is saying:

BEWARE – YOUR LIFE IS IN DANGER!!!

Don't envy people who are fearless. We tend to confuse fearlessness with bravery. My dictionary defines bravery as: able to face and endure danger. But if you have no fear how can you possibly be described as being brave? Surely bravery involves overcoming fear. If you have no fear of train journeys, for example, would you describe yourself as being brave because you travelled by train? Of course not.

I no longer have a fear of flying and therefore I don't regard myself as being particularly brave when I step on a plane. However, during the period when I was apprehensive, I was somewhat brave when I flew, and during the period that I was terrified, I was being very brave when I flew.

Soldiers or boxers are often described as being fearless. We tend to regard this description as being complimentary. In fact it is somewhat denigrating. If there was perceived danger, it doesn't matter whether the danger was real or merely possible. All normal and healthy creatures are programmed to feel fear when they sense danger. If you accidentally tread on a nail or lean against a hot stove, the resultant pain can be very unpleasant, and just as you might conclude how nice it would be to be fearless, you might conclude that it would be nice not to feel pain.

You would be wrong. The pain makes sure that you take your weight off that nail so that you don't drive it further into your foot, or jump away from that stove in order to limit the damage. Pain is your protection. However, there are people born without pain receptors. They are defective and abnormal and find it very difficult to survive. Because they feel no pain, they continue to lean on the hot stove and it's not until they can smell their flesh burning that they realize that something is wrong.

It's the same with fear. Some people are born lacking the imagination, sensitivity or intelligence either to anticipate danger or to recognize it even when it's jumping up and biting them on the nose. Such people are equally abnormal and deficient. Don't envy them. On the contrary – pity them. Eugine was fearless. Did he risk the lives of himself and his passengers because he was brave or because he was unimaginative, insensitive and unintelligent?

Should we admire and praise fearless people? No, we should pity them; all too often their lack of imagination, sensitivity and intelligence deprive them of their most precious gift – their lives – or cause them to spend the remainder of their lives crippled and mutilated.

You've no need to be ashamed of your fear of flying. It is a perfectly rational and natural instinct and I regard anyone who has never suffered from a fear of flying as a liar or a fool.

Now, you can be excused for thinking that I have contradicted myself. In Chapter 4 I categorically stated that a fear of flying is irrational. I'm now saying that FOF is a perfectly rational and natural instinct and that anyone who doesn't suffer from it is either a liar or a fool. No, I'm saying that anyone who has *never* suffered from it is either a liar or a fool.

You might consider this a rather rash statement to make, particularly when the accepted experts agree that only 20 per cent of fliers have a fear of flying. However, they all agree that the percentage might be much higher because many might not be prepared to admit to their fear.

The big Q cast some light on this subject. I asked an old friend if he knew anyone who suffered from FOF. He said yes, I do. His answer surprised me, partly because he didn't seem the type to be frightened of anything, and partly because I'd known him for over 40 years, knew that he flew regularly, yet I hadn't the slightest notion that he suffered from FOF.

The questionnaire revealed that his FOF didn't make him feel ashamed, cowardly, stupid or inferior. However, he did feel that it was irrational. I asked him why he felt it was irrational. He said:

"So many people tell me about the marvellous flight they had. Obviously most people find flying exhilarating so there must be something wrong with me!"

It occurred to me that during my "apprehensive" period, there was no way that I could have described any flight as exhilarating. However, I would often say: I had a marvellous flight. Was I being deceitful? No, what I meant was: there were no delays, there was no turbulence, the seats were comfortable, the food and service were excellent and for once my luggage wasn't the very last to be unloaded.

It is very important not just to accept the meaning of words verbatim, but to understand the context in which they are used. All heavy smokers envy casual smokers.

"Oh I can go all week without a cigarette, it doesn't bother me in the slightest!"

The heavy smoker accepts the statement and thinks:

"You lucky so and so, if only I could take it or leave it like that!"

However, if the casual smoker had said:

"Do you know, I can go all week without carrots!"

You'd think:

"That's a funny thing to say. Why on earth would he say something like that?"

The meaning of those words is to inform you that carrots present no problem to him. However, the fact that he finds it necessary to tell you so, belies the fact and implies the complete opposite. Why do smokers brag how little they smoke? When I was a golf addict, I would brag how often I could play and wanted to play more and more.

Casual smokers brag how little they smoke because they wish they didn't smoke at all, and when they tell you they can go a week without a cigarette, they are actually bragging – and so they should – because they've had to discipline themselves to go a whole week without cigarettes. What they are really telling you is that cigarettes are a problem to them.

I was ashamed to admit to my fear of boxing, my fear of spiders and my fear of flying. I've no doubt that I suffered from many other fears that I had been brainwashed into feeling ashamed to admit to.

We'll never know the true percentage of the population who have never suffered from a fear of flying. It doesn't matter. What I do know with absolute certainty is that anyone who has never suffered from it is to be pitied.

How can I expect you, whose sole object in reading this book is to be freed from the fear of flying, to pity someone who doesn't have it? Because the natural instinct for any physically and mentally healthy human being is to have a fear of flying and anyone who has never possessed it has a serious problem.

So if a fear of flying is a natural instinct, how can Allen Carr's method, or any other method for that matter, alter it?

Because although it is a natural instinct, it is still irrational. The deep end of a swimming pool is instinctively frightening to someone who cannot swim. Once they have learned to swim, the fear is irrational and that's why it disappears. However, drop that swimmer in the middle of the Atlantic and, no matter how competent that swimmer had become, the fear would become rational again.

Have you ever watched a bird encouraging its chicks to make their maiden flight? No one could doubt that a bird's natural instinct is to fly. At the same time it is equally obvious that even birds are apprehensive about that first flight.

The important factor is not whether it is instinctive or natural to fly, but whether it is safe. We need to accept that our natural instincts tell us that it is not safe.

Just as in my method to help smokers to quit, I don't waste time by telling them what they already know – the numerous and powerful reasons why they shouldn't smoke – I concentrate on the real problem: to remove the reasons that make them want to smoke. So what we need to achieve is not so much to convince you how safe it is to fly – you already know that. The real problem is to remove the factors that make you believe that it isn't.

Let's now examine in detail exactly why:

AN INITIAL FEAR OF FLYING IS BOTH NATURAL AND RATIONAL

8 An initial fear of flying is both natural and rational

When preparing the big Q I tried not to anticipate what the likely response to each question would be. However, I found it impossible not to do so. I was surprised that 67 per cent of the participants felt that FOF was a phobia. A phobia can be defined as an abnormal or irrational fear.

However, as I described earlier, fear is not an enemy but a friend. We've been talking about rational and irrational fears. Strictly speaking, fear itself can never be irrational. Fear is a warning against impending danger, which enables us to evade or remove the threat. It is a friend and essential to our survival. Even if it turns out that there was no real danger, the fear is still rational.

Let's take a simple example. When a captive silver-back gorilla first sees his reflection in a mirror, he is fooled into believing that his image is a rival and displays exactly the same fear and aggression as if he were confronted by a real rival. His behaviour is perfectly rational. Once he becomes familiar with the mirror he learns that there is no real threat. If he continued to react in the same way, his behaviour would be irrational. But he doesn't. The point I'm making is that fear is merely the rational reaction to a real or imaginary threat. Once you know that the threat is without foundation, the fear will automatically disappear.

You might argue:

> "I know flying is safe and I've actually been on several flights to prove it but I still have the fear."

The fact that you've survived several flights doesn't prove that flying is safe. In fact it can have the completely opposite effect. Some sufferers find the more they fly the worse it becomes. If you have a fear of flying it is because part of your brain still regards flying as either risky or unpleasant. Let's just go through the factors which lead me to believe that only a liar or a fool would not have an initial fear of flying. As an example I'll draw mainly, but not exclusively, from my own experience. Some of the points that I deal with might not relate to you. It makes no difference, you don't have to identify with all of them, but no doubt you will be able to identify with many of them. You might also be aware of additional points that apply in your case.

After 3 billion years of evolution and natural selection, the DNA of all creatures contains natural and instinctive fears which help them to survive. An essential one for most creatures is the fear of heights. It is what prevents fledglings from falling from the nest (those that do are usually pushed by their siblings) and makes us very cautious when climbing ladders because we know instinctively that to fall from a height is to suffer injury or even death. 35,000 ft is around the altitude that most modern commercial jets travel at. That is some considerable height. It is quite natural that we should feel fear when flying at that height, particularly when our instincts tell us that human beings aren't meant to fly. It's OK for birds, they are born with wings and only weigh a few ounces. But it contradicts our natural instincts that a huge hunk of metal weighing several tons, to which must be added the considerable weight of the fuel, passengers, crew and cargo, can defy the laws of gravity. If we were meant to fly, we would have wings.

The fear of death. Supposing the engines should fail. I can think of at least two occasions in my life when my car engine just cut out while I was travelling. Now, I'm not including times when it wouldn't start or when I had run out of petrol. On both occasions there was not the slightest element of danger and, consequently, no fear. However, you only need the engine to conk out once whilst airborne and you're dead!

The fear of claustrophobia. The interior of an aircraft can appear somewhat confined, particularly if it is full. The knowledge that the higher you go, the less oxygen there is, or that the cabin might be depressurized, can increase the feeling of claustrophobia. I've never suffered from claustrophobia but when those doors closed, I did suffer from a feeling that I interpreted as claustrophobia. It was the feeling of being trapped. The seat-belts, which ought to have relieved my anxiety, merely served to increase the feeling. I knew at this point that, no matter what trauma I would go through, I couldn't get off, I was trapped just as effectively as if I'd got my foot caught in a bear trap.

However, there were two even greater fears for me and I'm not sure which was the worse. The first was that at the two periods in the flight that I considered to be the most dangerous – take-off and landing – I wasn't allowed to smoke. At that time I believed that cigarettes were my courage and confidence, and to be deprived of them at the very times that I most needed them was a double blow.

Of course, at the time I didn't realize that, far from giving confidence and courage, smoking actually dissipates them. If you are a smoker, you will no doubt find this difficult to believe. Nevertheless, it is true and I've already spent enough time referring to smokers; if you want to know why smoking dissipates confidence and courage, you need to read *The Easy Way to Stop Smoking*.

The second major fear was that I was no longer in control. It wasn't just that my very life was now in the hands of some mustachioed, devil-may-care pilot, but also the mechanics, engineers and flight controllers.

Ironically, even the safety lecture prior to take-off, far from allaying my fears, actually increased them. Why was the stewardess explaining about the oxygen masks? It was obvious that she was expecting the plane to depressurize. Not only was she expecting it to depressurize, but she was expecting it to crash! Why else did she emphasize how important it was to know where the nearest emergency exit was? Not only were we going to crash, but we were actually going to ditch in the sea. Why else did we have life-jackets under our seats?

Yet another fear is FIRE! A fire on the ground is bad enough, but how does the fire brigade reach you at 35,000 ft?

My worst fear was bad weather and turbulence. I've always hated fairground rides. The thought of those awful air pockets when your stomach remains at 35,000 ft whilst the plane and the rest of your body drops to 34,000 ft in a matter of seconds, was my worst nightmare.

With the exception of air pockets, which don't actually exist, all of the above fears are natural, rational and an inherent part of our make-up. In addition to our instinctive fears, we have been subjected to massive brainwashing from birth. I was born in 1934. My first knowledge of flying was the Battle of Britain. A pilot's life was measured in weeks. OK, so they were trying to shoot each other out of the sky, but I was not left with the impression that flying was the safest form of transport and today you don't even need to shoot the plane out of the sky, you have terrorists and hijackers who are only too willing to place a bomb on the plane.

Commercial flying was in its infancy in those days. I cannot tell you what the actual statistics were, but I did regard defying the laws of gravity as a highly risky pastime. It's now over 40 years since man first ventured into space. There have been relatively few accidents, but I still perceive going to the moon as a highly risky venture and you'd have to force me screaming into a rocket in order to get me there.

However, the most destructive and powerful form of brainwashing, which increases our natural and instinctive fears, comes from the media. They give the impression that every day, somewhere in the world, airplanes are falling out of the sky, crashing into mountains, colliding with each other, running out of fuel, ditching into the ocean, being hijacked or blown up by terrorists, suffering metal fatigue or mechanical failure, being flown by alcoholics, drug addicts or badly trained crews, being maintained with faulty replacement parts, going off course, being pounded by hurricane-force gales or struck by lightning, being threatened by ice, flocks of birds, dust storms or whatever.

Closely following the media are the many Hollywood fantasies, supposedly based partially on fact, about air disasters. I'm sure you are aware of what I mean. The captain has marital problems and isn't really concentrating on the flight. The co-pilot is a secret alcoholic and keeps nipping off for crafty swigs on his flask. The senior stewardess is a nymphomaniac and only got the job because she obliged her assessors. The flight controller has a drug problem. One of the passengers is a terrorist and has deposited a bomb on the plane. Another is eight months pregnant and is now in the advanced stages of labour. A third passenger is found to be suffering from a highly contagious infection and unless he receives the correct medication the whole of Western society will be infected. The destination airport is fogbound, as is every other airport within 500 miles and the instruments reveal a leak in the fuel tank. At this point number-one engine breaks down, followed a few minutes later by number two. To cap it all, the hydraulics have failed and the undercarriage cannot be released.

No doubt you think that I exaggerate. Of course I do, but so does Hollywood. The point is that it is all conceivable. Practically every situation that I have described has actually happened sometime on a flight. It doesn't matter that the odds of them all happening on the same flight would include so many noughts that this book wouldn't be large enough to contain them.

The truth is that we are affected by these films. In fact, as we watch them in the safety of our living rooms, we undergo a reduced version of the anxiety that the crew and passengers are suffering. When the captain finally completes the miracle landing, we share the release of tension and feel like cheering him like the passengers in the film.

Whether I'm trying to cure smokers, over-eaters, alcoholics, heroin addicts or FOF, what I'm actually trying to do is remove fear. At the smoking clinics our clients arrive in various stages of panic; like fearful fliers they don't like to admit it, nevertheless it's blatantly obvious to us. An important part of my method is to relax them and there is no better agent than to introduce humour. However, with FOF, even the jokes tend to exacerbate the problem rather than solve it:

> "There were two Irishman on a return flight to Dublin. Beep: if you care to look out of the starboard window, you will notice that the starboard engine is no longer working. However, this is no cause for alarm. This plane is a TriStar. It has three engines and can fly and land safely on one engine. However, the loss of power means that the flight will be delayed by 30 minutes. 30 minutes later: Beep: if you care to look out of the port window, you will notice that the port engine has also broken down. But as I explained earlier, this is no cause for alarm, this plane can land perfectly safely on one engine. However, the flight will be delayed by a further 30 minutes. One Irishman turned to the other and said: I hope that third engine doesn't break down, otherwise we'll be up here all night."

I must first apologize to the Irish. My only defence is that the joke was told to me by an Irishman. When I heard the joke I was quite encouraged to learn that a TriStar could safely fly and land on one engine. But I didn't believe it. Why would a TriStar have three engines if it only needed one? The joke also suggests that it is mathematically possible for two engines to break down within half an hour of each other.

Of all the jokes that I have heard about flying, that is the one that creates the least fear of flying. Another is about the instructor who takes a trainee pilot 50 yards above Brighton beach at 600 mph:

Instructor: I bet half the people down there thought we'd had an accident.

Trainee: Half the people up here *have* had an accident!

The joke that confirmed my worst fears was the one about the $10 Charter Tours economy flight to Florida:

> "We sat in this old Dakota that still had the bullet holes from WW2, waiting for the pilot. Then this character in a peaked cap, gold braid, a white stick and dark glasses was being led to the plane by a guide dog:
> "Is that the captain?"
> "He's the best in the business."
> "But he's blind! How does he know when to take off?"
> "He has incredibly acute hearing. He guns it down the runway and when he can hear, above the roar of the engines, the passengers shout KIN'ELL, he know's it's time to lift off."

Exaggerated it may be, but my first flight was a charter flight and the joke did nothing to allay my fears.

Perhaps the worst exaggerators are the frightened fliers themselves. A typical example of media exaggeration increased by passenger confirmation was:

> "Plane plunges 25,000 ft after depressurization!"

What actually happened was that the pressurization equipment broke down. The oxygen masks dropped as they are programmed to do. The passengers were comfortable and perfectly able to breathe. The captain, after checking with air-traffic control, made a rapid but controlled descent to 7,000 ft. It was only natural that the passengers would dramatize the situation. Wouldn't you and I do the same thing? The captain was described as a hero. He was very modest:

"I only did what I was trained to do."

In fact he described the incident exactly as it happened. The plane didn't plunge a single foot, there was no panic. Both he and the aircraft were in control throughout the incident. It was purely routine. But the media aren't interested in routine flights. There's no news value in routine flights and if there is no news, you have to create some.

In the big Q, only 11 per cent of the participants were ashamed of their fear of flying and only 22 per cent thought it was cowardly; 56 per cent thought it was irrational but only 33 per cent thought it stupid; 44 per cent actually thought they were inferior to people who didn't suffer from a fear of flying and 67 per cent regarded it as a phobia.

Now I would ask you to re-read from the beginning of this chapter. The several instinctive fears involved in flying are both natural and real. The massive brainwashing that we have been bombarded with by the media and Hollywood is also real. To these must be added the brainwashing, misconceptions and faulty information we receive from friends, colleagues and society generally. Wouldn't you agree with me that anyone who has never had a fear of flying is either a liar or a fool?

You have absolutely no need to feel ashamed, stupid or inferior and while you still have misconceptions about flying, your fear isn't a phobia but perfectly rational. If you've already flown in spite of your fear, you certainly have no reason to feel cowardly. If you've never plucked up enough courage to fly or, having once flown, can no longer do so, this does not necessarily mean that you are less courageous. It might only mean that you have more sensitivity, or more imagination, so that your fear is greater. It might also mean that your need or desire to fly is not so great as that of others. It might also mean that you are less brave. It's impossible to tell.

The point is, we don't need to know. The object of this book isn't to make you brave so that you can overcome your fears or to provide you with techniques that will help you to cope with them. Even if I were able to do that, I wouldn't. My desire isn't to enable you to spend the rest of your life white-knuckling it from one city or country to another.

My sole object is to remove those fears entirely so that you can actually enjoy flying. Just as the gorilla's initial reaction to the mirror was instinctive and natural, so are the several fears connected with flying, but the beautiful truth is that they represent no more threat to you than the mirror does to the gorilla. Now, I don't mean that I'm going to try to persuade you or kid you; the aircraft industry has already tried to convince you that flying is completely safe and it has already convinced the majority of fliers. However, you aren't quite as gullible as they were, you won't be satisfied until you have convinced yourself.

I've said that flying is completely safe. Am I really saying that the industry has reached a stage where accidents are impossible? Of course not. What I'm saying is that today flying is so safe that once you know all the facts it will be as irrational for you to fear it as for the gorilla that realizes he is merely looking at his own reflection. Let's use some examples.

Do you lie awake at night worrying that you are going to die from a kick by a donkey? Of course you don't. Yet more people are killed or injured each year from donkey kicks than from flying. A true but surprising statistic. However, perhaps you think it somewhat misleading in that you have no need or intention of getting within kicking distance of a donkey, whereas you do want to fly.

OK, let's use another example. When you step into your garden do you do so with trepidation and a fear of doom? Over 70 UK citizens died from accidents in the garden during 1997 and another half million suffered accidents that required hospital treatment. This does not include death from heart attacks or similar causes. In spite of the fact that the average UK citizen spends many more hours in their garden than they do flying, throughout the whole of 1997, in respect of flights involved in public-transport facilities:

THERE WAS NOT A SINGLE ACCIDENT OR FATALITY IN THE UK!

No doubt you suspect that I've picked 1997 because it was a particularly safe year? It's not possible to get any safer. But I could have chosen 1988, or 1990, or 1991, or 1992, or 1996. They aren't in the minority, they are the norm! In each of those years:

THERE WAS NOT A SINGLE ACCIDENT OR FATALITY IN THE UK!

Apart from a walk in your garden, there are many other examples I could use. You could be excused for suspecting that I'm using this particular example to convince you just how safe flying is. You would be wrong. I'm using it to demonstrate that even with the threat of serious accident or death we can still enter our gardens with a feeling of pleasure rather than doom and gloom.

I should also make it absolutely clear that this work and any statistics that I quote relate only to normal business, pleasure or holiday jet flights, including charter flights, departing from Western Europe, North America or Australasia. It includes return flights from anywhere in the world provided

the return flight is with the same airline as the outward flight. I
will refer to such flights as being within:

"THE LIMITATIONS"

It is important that you remember "THE LIMITATIONS",
because I shall be referring to this phrase frequently. One of the
main causes of our fear of flying is the massive brainwashing that
we receive from the media and Hollywood. Whether we like it or
not, we are both consciously and subconsciously affected by this
brainwashing. The vast majority of disasters, or near disasters,
reported by the media are not only exaggerated, speculative and
dramatized, but relate to flights outside "THE LIMITATIONS".

Hollywood exaggerates outrageously and unfortunately
tends to do it about flights within "THE LIMITATIONS".
Hollywood is fiction! Even so, we are still affected both
consciously and subconsciously. We need to remove the effects of
this brainwashing and deal in hard facts.

"THE LIMITATIONS" do not include helicopters, hot-air
balloons, airships, military aircraft, single-engined planes,
privately owned planes or any form of glider, or airlines flying
from outside the locations that I have indicated.

Does this imply that it is dangerous to fly in helicopters,
hot-air balloons or with airlines or from locations outside "THE
LIMITATIONS"? Dangerous is a relative term. All I can tell you
is that in the period after I had lost my dread of flying, but was
still apprehensive, I did a helicopter flight around Manhattan
island with some apprehension and a hot-air-balloon flight
above Lake Tahoe, which was a pleasure from take-off to landing.

For most of us, helicopter flights and hot-air-balloon
flights are not essential and the quality of our lives is not greatly
affected if we don't wish to take them. The object of this book is
to enable people whose lives are being seriously and adversely
affected, because they are too frightened to use the cheapest,

quickest and safest method of travelling comparatively long distances, or who do so, but find the experience ranges from severe apprehension to out-and-out terror.

After you have learned to enjoy flights within "THE LIMITATIONS", you might well decide to travel on flights outside them, or to fly in helicopters or hot-air balloons. I do not wish to imply that the locations and types of flying machine excluded are unsafe. It is merely that this book is designed to enable readers who wish to enjoy such flights as I have included in "THE LIMITATIONS", to realize that those flights are absolutely safe. My research is therefore limited to those flights.

Your third instruction was to start off in a happy frame of mind. It occurs to me that the contents of this chapter might well have curbed your enthusiasm. However, it was essential to be aware of the causes of your FOF and that they are not the result of deficiencies in your character or make-up.

Society tends to regard smokers as weak-willed, inconsiderate and rather stupid people with disgusting, anti-social habits. Having been a chain-smoker for over 30 years I couldn't contradict this image. It wasn't until I escaped from the slavery that I was able to see smokers in their true light.

I had similar misgivings about my fear of flying. I felt weak, cowardly, irrational and stupid. It wasn't until I lost the fear that I could see the true position clearly. My experience with smoking should have taught me better, but I confess I was surprised to discover that several of my friends and acquaintances, people whom I'd known for years, physically and mentally strong, and intelligent achievers, were also cursed with FOF. From the information provided by the participants of the big Q it soon became obvious that people suffering from FOF were not just irrational jellyfish. The vast majority comprised rational and intelligent people.

From this point on I want you to dispel all negative thoughts. From this you might deduce that my method is merely an exercise in positive thinking. Not so. I've been a natural positive thinker all my life, but that didn't enable me to lose my fear of flying. I didn't even lose it when I understood the exact reasons for that fear. I lost it when I understood exactly why those reasons were without foundation.

I suppose the most typical example of positive thinking is the traditional pep talk that the American football coach gives his team before the kick-off of the big match:

> "We're gonna go in there and destroy them. We'll pulverize them! We'll kill them because we're the best!"

I'd be sitting there thinking:

> "Does he think I'm stupid? The other coach is saying exactly the same thing but one team has to lose!"

To me such a pep talk isn't positive thinking, but stupid thinking. To me a positive pep talk would be:

> "We've analysed several weaknesses in their defence that we can exploit. We've studied their strategies in attack, learned exactly how they score their points and devised counter-strategies. We're just as big and heavy as they are but we've trained so that we're twice as fit. We've practised our skills and strategies and got them down to perfection. We're a team, a well-oiled machine, there's no way we can lose. Go out and enjoy yourselves."

Now that's really positive thinking, not based on just hope, luck or determination, but on solid fact. You could argue that perhaps the other team have used exactly the same techniques and will outsmart you. You are absolutely correct but let's continue with the football analogy.

Let's assume that you are better than the other team in every department of the game. Your team is bigger, stronger, fitter, more agile and more intelligent. You have superior tactics in both defence and attack and your quarter-back and kicker are twice as good as your opponents'. How could you lose? I would suggest that there is only one way that you could possibly lose. That is, instead of coming on to the field full of confidence, you didn't believe in yourselves. You were so overawed by the reputation of the other team that you came onto the pitch in a state of panic and just capitulated to the other side. In other words you lost, not because you weren't capable, but because of negative thinking.

This is the exact situation that you are in:

THERE IS NO OTHER TEAM

Or rather, the other team is merely a series of instincts and beliefs that are misconceptions and illusions.

THAT IS THE FACT OF THE MATTER

One by one we are going to destroy those misconceptions. Although my method isn't just an exercise in positive thinking, nevertheless, it is essential that you:

THINK POSITIVELY

And that is your fourth instruction. Keep a happy frame of mind, remember you have absolutely nothing to lose and so much to gain and that all the advantages are on your side.

Let's begin by exploding the first myth:

IF WE WERE MEANT TO FLY, WE'D BE BORN WITH WINGS

9 If we were meant to fly, we ~~were born~~ with wings

The fact that something appears to be un~~natural~~ ~~doesn't~~ preclude us from participating in it without fear ~~or enjoyment.~~ We weren't born with wheels, skis or surfboards. Come to that, we weren't born with houses, boats, trains, televisions or telephones. Unlike the tortoise, we weren't even born with a house on our back and there's certainly nothing natural about this computer that I sit and stare at every day, but I'd sure be lost without it.

Another surprise that came from the big Q was that trains were the least frightening of the other modes of transport. Yet trains could hardly be described as a natural form of transport. We weren't born with wheels but are quite happy to build our own, so why aren't we just as happy to build our own wings in the form of airplanes?

I believe it's because, although cars and trains might not be natural, they do not appear to defy the laws of nature. Our natural knowledge of flying is confined to certain creatures, mainly birds, which are incredibly light and flap their wings. Perhaps Sir Isaac Newton was the first to define the law of gravity, but from time immemorial, creatures on this planet soon learned that what went up must come down, and the heavier the creature and the higher it went up, the bigger the thump when it came down.

I'm certain that this is the basic key to our fear of flying. Our every instinct cries out that it is impossible for a huge lump of metal weighing several tons to hurtle through the sky at 500 mph without coming down with a huge bump. It seems natural. It defies every law of nature, not least of Newton's law, and anyone who is stupid enough untarily to ride in that lump of metal has only themselves to blame if they are terrified.

The truth is that, far from defying the laws of nature, an airplane, like a sail boat, is in complete harmony with them. Before we consider the problem of how a large aircraft can take off and stay in the air, let's consider an even bigger problem: how do you keep modern racing cars and power-boats on the ground? After all, they are also heavy metal objects. A modern commercial jet takes off and lands at speeds in the region of 150 mph.

At such speeds even cars have a tendency to take off. We've all seen pictures of power-boats flying through the air after the bow has come up too high. Fast cars and boats have to be aeronautically designed to prevent them from taking off. Many modern cars are fitted with spoilers to help keep them on the ground.

If ever you've worn a hat on a windy day, particularly if it has even a small brim, you'll know that no matter how firmly you ram it on to your head, unless you hold your head down and face into the breeze, that hat will lift off and go flying through the air, and it doesn't take a particularly strong wind to do it. If it's a wide-brimmed hat, the problem is compounded. A mere zephyr is sufficient to create absolute chaos on Ladies' Day at Royal Ascot.

Now, the main object of the Ascot creations is purely aesthetic and it is indeed unfortunate that they tend to possess aeronautical characteristics. However, a modern jet plane is designed to take the greatest advantage of this perfectly natural phenomenon.

From time immemorial, mankind has envied the birds. The first attempts to emulate them were to manufacture wings that flapped. Needless to say, those first attempts were unsuccessful, dangerous and often disastrous. It's difficult to believe that it is less than 100 years since Orville and Wilbur made that inaugural flight. Initially we learned much from the birds. However, our knowledge of aeronautics has increased by momentous proportions since that time. We have learned from an immense amount of practical experiences, aided by modern communications and computers.

Think of the vast surface area on the wings of a modern jet plane as the wide brim of a hat; those wings are so shaped that a head-on wind of sufficient speed will make them lift, and just as the brim of a hat sends the whole hat flying through the air, so when the wings of an airplane lift, the rest of the plane has no choice but to lift with then.

But a hat flying through the air is a very unstable affair and is subject to the vagaries of the wind. When the wind drops, the hat crashes, no matter how wide the brim. This is true. But an airplane has several major advantages over a hat. The first is that it creates its own wind. I remember when I first took up jogging, the outward journey would always be against the wind. I quite liked the idea. It meant that on the return journey, when I was more tired, the wind would be at my back. It was amazing and typical of Sod's Law, the moment I turned for home, the wind direction would not only change, but be the complete reverse.

For those who are not familiar with Sod's Law, I regret my dictionary fails even to recognize it. This is a serious omission because it's by far the most important law of nature. However, a couple of examples will suffice. Take the law of averages: if you spin a coin many times, the number of times it lands heads will be very similar to the number of times it lands tails. However, if you have gambled on the result, it will always land the opposite to whatever you chose – that's Sod's Law. Another example is when you drop your toast: it will not only always land marmalade-side down, but always on a thick-piled carpet, never on tiles. There are people who have devoted their whole lives to dropping pieces of toast; there is not a single authenticated case in the history of mankind of a slice of toast landing marmalade-side up. Sod's Law is far more powerful than the law of averages.

It was some time before it dawned on me that when you run in any direction, you have to overcome the resistance of the air, so even if there is no wind whatsoever there always appears to be. The jet engines thrust the aircraft forward; the greater the speed it goes forward, the greater the air resistance and, depending on the weight and design of the aircraft, when it reaches a certain speed, it has no choice but to lift off.

Am I saying that is what happens on a take-off, the pilot keeps accelerating until the plane lifts off? No I'm not, I'm merely describing the principles of flight. It isn't a miracle that several hundred tons of metal can lift off the ground and remain in the air, it's one of the natural principles of nature; the plane has no choice but to follow those laws. In fact it would be a miracle if it didn't!

The second major advantage that the plane has over the hat is that, not only does it create its own wind, but it has complete control over the speed and direction of the wind that it creates at all times. That wind, which I will now refer to as thrust, only drops if and when the pilot wants it to drop and will do so at the rate and time that the pilot orders it to.

That's all very well but surely a plane must be affected by the vagaries of normal winds and how can you compare the weight of a hat with several hundred tons of metal?

The thrust of just one modern jet engine is many times more powerful than the most powerful hurricane. Cars and houses are very heavy and are designed to remain on terra firma; even so, you've probably seen pictures of them being picked up and tossed by a tornado as if they were matchboxes. An aircraft is affected by normal winds, but its own thrust is so powerful that those winds become relatively insignificant and the plane can make adjustment for them anyway.

The third major advantage that the plane holds over the hat is that the hat is not only dependent on a wind in order to fly and subject to the vagaries of that wind, but it has no control over its own shape. The same brim that sent it flying into the air can send it crashing into the ground. Any inexperienced kite flyer will know the experience. You wait for a gust of wind, your hopes rise as the kite soars to 20 ft and are dashed as the next instant it crashes into the ground. I'm certain that such experiences also tend to contribute to a fear of flying. After all, if a kite that is light and designed to remain airborne crashes at a speed as if it were constructed of metal, what chance has an aircraft that weighs several hundred tons?

Unfortunately for the kite, it suffers from the same disadvantage as the hat, it cannot change its shape. Am I suggesting that modern jet planes can actually change their shape? That is exactly what I am suggesting and that is exactly what they do. Now, the changes may not appear to be substantial; indeed, they are so relatively slight that many fliers aren't even aware of their existence. But the changes don't need to be substantial. The brim of a hat might be the perfect shape to make it lift off, but the overall shape of the hat will make that flight very erratic.

An arrow or a dart is the ideal shape to send it unerringly to its target, but make one slight alteration, remove the flight, and the effect is catastrophic. In fact the tail of an airplane is like the flight of a dart. It is one of the chief stabilizing characteristics that ensure that the plane has to fly forwards and upright.

Unlike the hat, the airplane's shape is designed specifically to lift off and to remain stable throughout the flight. I know it can be difficult to believe that a metal object weighing several hundred tons can lift off and remain airborne. I've given a very simplistic explanation of how and why it does happen. Actually we don't need to prove that it can happen, we know it happens. It has been estimated that at any moment there are over half a million aircraft airborne.

However, it helps to know how and why they can remain airborne to understand why modern civil jets are so safe. The true reason is not just their basic design, or the immense power of their engines, but their ability to change shape, their ability to be in complete control throughout the flight. Not surprisingly this phenomenon is known as the controls.

Possibly the best way to demonstrate this point is to describe:

A TYPICAL TAKE-OFF

10 A typical take-off

In the bad old days, I used to divide every flight into four distinct phases of terror:

1 The take-off on the outward flight.
2 The landing on the outward flight.
3 The take-off on the return flight.
4 The landing on the return flight.

Why did I do this? Because society had brainwashed me into believing that the take-off and landing were the most dangerous periods of the flight.

My first design of the big Q included two questions which I subsequently omitted:

1 Do you believe that flying is the safest form of transport?
2 What do you believe Is the most dangerous stage of the flight?

Ironically the answer to the first question was invariably yes. Equally invariably the answer to the second question would be the landing or the take-off. Why is this ironic? Because although each answer appears to be correct, they contradict each other. If flying is safe, how can landings and take-offs be described as dangerous? In fact it is the wording of question 2 that causes the anomaly. Landings and take-offs are not dangerous and the truth is: no stage of the flight is dangerous.

However, because the relatively few accidents that occur

often happen either during take-off or landing, our brains are fooled into believing that these manoeuvres are actually dangerous. They are no more dangerous than the starting-up or stopping of a train. The wording of question 2 gives the impression that flying is in fact dangerous.

Even after I had learned to cope with flying, my wife and I would hold hands throughout take-off and landing. And when each take-off or landing was completed without disaster, we I would smile at each other as if we had survived an avalanche or a hurricane. Why did we do this? After all, we don't go through a similar ritual on any other form of transport. I knew why I did it. It was because I truly believed that I'd survived some risky experience. But why did Joyce, who claims she has never suffered from FOF, have the need to do it?

We still go through the same ritual today. I cannot speak for Joyce, but I do it, not because I have any fear of take-off or landing, but because it's become a nice, endearing habit and it does remind me of the times that I would not so much be holding her hand as breaking her fingers. Joyce says the reason that she isn't frightened of flying is that if we die, at least we die together. I find that both comforting and flattering, but the mere fact that we don't do it when getting on a bus or a train means that she believes that the odds of our dying when taking off or landing must be far greater.

Let's now explain why the controls make a take-off so incredibly safe. You have safely taxied to the main runway. The engines are already running and have just been serviced, as has the rest of the plane. The captain increases the thrust of the engines and then lets off the brakes. You start accelerating down the runway. You reach a speed at which you instinctively feel that the plane ought to lift off. But it doesn't. You sense that something is wrong. This is when you begin to regret that you packed the golf clubs and to wonder whether you will run out of runway. You find yourself actually trying physically to lift up the plane. You feel like shouting out to all the other passengers:

> "Come on! If we all concentrate hard enough we can get this thing off the ground."

In all probability your sensations were correct, the pilot could have lifted off at the speed you sensed. So why didn't he? Because he is just as keen to survive as you are.

The exact speed that the pilot should pull back on that stick is computed in advance. The airline doesn't just weigh your luggage in order to extract more money from you in the form of an excess-baggage charge. It knows the unladen weight of the aircraft, but it also needs to know the number of passengers and crew and the weight of the cargo and fuel. From this it can compute the exact speed the plane needs to travel at in order to lift off.

However, to lift off at this speed could be very risky: a slight miscalculation or change in external wind conditions, or a fault developing in one of the engines at the exact moment of lift-off might cause the plane to stall. So the pilot doesn't even attempt to lift off at this speed. As with every other aspect of modern civil aviation a safety margin is built in. In the case of take-off speed this safety margin is about 30 per cent. So if the actual take-off speed were 150 mph this means that the pilot could have lifted off at about 115 mph.

How does the pilot keep the plane on the ground when the laws of aeronautics dictate that it should lift off at 115 mph? This is where the control or change of shape comes into it. Both the wings and the tail have parts that move. Let's just refer to them as the flaps. Think of the wide-brimmed hat. If the brim slopes downwards, it is less likely to lift from your head. If it slopes upwards, any number of hat pins won't hold it on.

For the initial part of the take-off, the pilot uses the flaps like the spoilers on a car, to keep the aircraft on the ground.

When he reaches the speed at which he knows that nothing can prevent the plane from lifting off, he merely reverses the flaps and the plane has no choice but to obey the laws of nature and go flying upwards.

The plane has been serviced before it taxis to the runway. The pilot has a wide, flat runway all to himself. He accelerates to the pre-computed lift-off speed, pulls back the lever and the plane has no choice but to fly upwards. What can possibly go wrong?

I'm sure you can think of many things. During the next few chapters we'll discuss them. Perhaps the biggest and most common fear is:

ENGINE FAILURE

11 Engine failure

I estimate that I've driven about half a million miles in my lifetime and, apart from running out of petrol, I can recall only two occasions when the engine conked out while I was actually driving. That's an average of once in a quarter of a million miles. I think that is a great compliment to the reliability of the average car engine, particularly when you consider that in the early days I could only afford bangers and couldn't afford to service them.

However, I believe this was the basis of my fear of flying. It only needs to happen once while airborne, the plane will drop like a stone and you are dead. Now, a modern jet engine is less complicated than the normal car engine. It has fewer moving parts and is inherently more reliable. It is also serviced after every flight and removed from service at regular intervals for a complete overhaul. If there is the slightest suspicion that an engine has a fault, by the mechanics, the flight engineer or the pilot, the plane will not attempt to take off.

The average rate of failure per mile of a modern jet engine within "THE LIMITATIONS" is less than once in 10 million miles. The majority of pilots do not experience a single example of engine failure throughout their entire careers.

However reassuring these statistics might be, there are two other far more important factors of safety. The most important is that all jet aircraft are designed to fly and land safely on just one engine. Even if the jet has four engines it can fly and land safely on just one engine!

Going back to my car analogy, if I'd had two engines in

the car, I would only have broken down once in 625,000,000 miles. I would have to have lived until I was 700,000 years old in order to break down just once. This is longer than the human race has existed on this planet! If you were the first human being to exist on this planet and had eternal life, you could have flown from the moment you were born until the year AD 2000, without once having experienced two engines breaking down at the same time. The chances are more than one in 100,000,000,000,000 and you'd have to live until you were 100,000 million years old. That's over a hundred thousand times longer than man has existed on this planet. Since all the aircraft included in "THE LIMITATIONS" will have two or more engines, I think you will agree with me that engine failure is really no cause for alarm.

But supposing one engine fails at the critical moment of lift-off? Even in that 1-in-10-million possibility, remember that the plane already possesses more speed than it needs to lift off safely; the remaining engine, or engines, is or are quite capable of keeping the plane in the air. However, there is this second important factor: an airplane, no matter how much it weighs, will not just drop like a stone the moment that the power is cut off.

Just think of Evel Knievel clearing 20 double-decker buses on his motor bike. A motor bike moves forward by its wheels having traction with the ground. So the moment the ground is no longer there, it has the same effect as if his engine had cut out. Now a motor bike and its rider are relatively heavy objects and are designed to stay on the ground, but do they drop like a stone? No way, their impetus keeps them airborne.

Coincidentally, today the media broke the news of a private aircraft whose single engine failed. The pilot glided 40 miles to complete a safe landing at the nearest airport. Needless to say, the general impression given was of a miraculous escape. It was no miracle. Airplanes are designed to glide. The space shuttle actually glides to a safe landing after re-entry into the atmosphere. Even if all four engines of a large modern jet were to fail at the same time, at 35,000 ft it could glide for nearly 200 miles and complete a perfectly safe landing. Airplanes do not drop like a stone even when the thrust is cut off completely.

If the instruments indicate any fault, be it mechanical or otherwise, or should a fault become apparent during take-off but prior to lift-off, the pilot will abort the take-off. But is the runway long enough for him to abort safely? The simple answer to that is yes. As with every other aspect of modern commercial aviation, a huge safety margin is allowed for.

In fact it would pay you to visit your nearest international airport. Most of them provide adequate viewing areas for the public. Take the children with you and treat it as an exciting day out. The temptation is to pick a nice day. Don't, instead pick a day when the weather is such that you think flying might be risky, when it's windy and raining. Watch plane after plane take off or land safely without any histrionics. In particular, notice how comparatively little of the total length of the runway even the largest jets need to use whether they are taking off or landing. After a couple of hours the whole business becomes mundane and rather boring.

If a fault occurs after lift-off, the pilot will either land immediately or, if a fault occurs later in the flight, he will land at the nearest available airport.

But there are many other mechanical things that can go wrong apart from engine failure. What about the hydraulics; surely the undercarriage and flaps depend on hydraulics? What happens if there's a fault in the hydraulics? You've been watching those war films again. Of course these things depend upon hydraulics, but just as with the engines, any vital safety function of an aircraft is duplicated, triplicated or sometimes quadrupled. The hydraulics are a classic example. The controls are worked from three separate systems, each one of which is capable of working them alone. Even should all three malfunction at the same time, there is an emergency system which will enable the plane to fly and land safely.

Now, I'm sure that there are many similar points that you can think of. Stop worrying, if you've thought of them, so have the professionals and, if they are vital, the system will be duplicated and triplicated if necessary. But:

WHAT HAPPENS IF A WING FALLS OFF?

12   What happens if a wing falls off?

In all probability you will die. It's never happened yet and probably never will. We are now entering the realms of fantasy. Even so, I have to admit that this used to bother me. I think it was because I could actually see the wing moving. No, I'm not talking about the flaps or the slats; I knew they were meant to move. I'm talking about the whole wing. I'm supposed to be sitting in a fixed-wing aircraft yet I can see the wing flexing. I never realized that the wings were designed to flex and that it was a vital part of their strength. Picture a weeping willow in a storm. Its branches will bend with the wind but they won't break, whereas the more rigid branches of other trees will snap.

Like every other vital factor in the construction of an aircraft, the wings are subjected to stresses many times greater than those they could possibly experience during actual flights. To worry about a wing becoming detached at 500 mph is equivalent to worrying about your arm becoming detached in a wind of 10 miles per hour. It just cannot happen.

I've confessed that I did once have those worries and it was usually during a period which also used to strike terror into my heart:

TURBULENCE

13   Turbulence

What is turbulence? It occurs when the external air currents are colliding and become erratic. It most commonly occurs when going into cloud cover after take-off or before landing or during bad weather.

The effect of turbulence is that the flight ceases to be completely smooth. It can range in intensity from a slight vibration to actual buffeting of the aircraft. At the lower range it is no more uncomfortable than driving a car over cat's-eyes. In the middle range I would describe it as like driving over cobblestones, or being mounted on a horse that is trotting when you can't get into the rhythm. At its worst I would describe it as like being in a small boat on a choppy sea.

Occasionally turbulence occurs when there's not a cloud in the sky. This is known as clear-air turbulence or CAT. I found it more frightening on those occasions than I did when travelling through cloud or bad weather. The reason was that I believed the vibration was caused not by air currents but because something had gone wrong with the plane itself.

Like most aspects of flying, it wasn't so much the turbulence itself that worried me, but the belief that we were in danger. I've now completed over 200 flights in my life. I believe that every one of those flights included periods of slight turbulence. At times it was so slight as to be hardly noticeable except for the rings on my coffee cup.

Only once have I experienced severe turbulence. For someone like me, who hated fairground rides, it was a genuinely unpleasant experience. This was when I would look at the wings, see them flexing and believe that we were genuinely going through a dangerous experience.

I promise you that turbulence represents no more threat to a modern jet plane than those cobblestones do to your car. Uncomfortable as it might be, there is not one single accident in the history of modern aviation that has been caused by turbulence. Uncomfortable it may be:

DANGEROUS IT IS NOT!

I find it impossible to analyse how much of my previous hatred of turbulence was due to the actual physical annoyance and how much to my fear of the illusory danger. All I can tell you is that since I lost the fear, turbulence has no more bothered me than driving over cobblestones.

It might also help you to know that modern jets are equipped with radar, whose function is not only to avoid other aircraft and mountains, but to avoid bad weather. If a plane were to be struck by lightning it would not damage the aircraft or the contents. However, the radar can detect bad weather 400 miles ahead. The pilot will avoid bad weather and turbulence, not because it represents any danger to the aircraft, but because he and his bosses are dedicated professionals and want to provide you with the most pleasant flight possible.

Every flight has a pre-arranged flight plan, which we will discuss later. One of the features of that plan is to avoid bad weather. If weather patterns change during the flight, the pilot will radio flight control in order to avoid bad weather, and flight control, who are also experienced professionals, dedicated to ensuring that you enjoy the flight, will do their best to revise the flight plan in order to avoid the bad weather. However, they will only do so providing it is safe to do so.

In every aspect of the aircraft industry:

SAFETY COMES FIRST!

Your comfort comes second but it comes a long way behind safety. That is because we are the customer and there have been several studies about this subject. In every one of those studies, passengers are unanimous that they would rather pay extra than risk their safety. Incidentally, so would the crews.

Clear-air turbulence is difficult to detect. Fortunately it is rare and, because there is a continual exchange of information between aircraft and flight control, in all probability it will have been reported by a previous aircraft and so be avoided.

Joyce and I are fortunate to have a circle of friends that enjoy a meal out accompanied by lively music. For most of the evening we are content to act our age and watch the youngsters enjoying themselves. Eventually a song from our youth will be struck up. Something like:

SHAKE, RATTLE AND ROLL, or

THE HIPPY, HIPPY SHAKE

We have no more chance of remaining seated than that Ascot hat has of remaining on the beauty's head. We'll show these youngsters what dancing is really about. We jump and gyrate around the floor, inflicting more punishment on our poor old bones than we're ever likely to suffer during the severest turbulence.

Any budding equestrian will know the feeling that I described earlier. The stupid animal isn't even galloping, but when it goes up, your butt is coming down and vice versa. It's the same when trying to jive with someone whose rhythm is diametrically opposed to your own. But what an exhilarating experience it is when you learn to trot in harmony with the horse or jive in harmony with your partner.

It's exactly the same with turbulence; you can fight it and feel uncomfortable, or you can learn to ride or dance with it. After all, there's no danger, it's either shake, rattle and roll or you do the hippy, hippy shake, or whatever similar song you want to play in your mind. Provided you keep your seat-belt on, the very worst thing that can happen to you during turbulence is that you spill some of your drink.

It is severe turbulence that has created this myth about air pockets. The myth really goes back to the days of propeller flights. The plane plunges several feet. The obvious explanation is that it has encountered a vacuum. There is nothing for the propellers to grip on in order to keep the aircraft aloft.

Now we already know from the "Evcl Knievel" comparison that even with air resistance, the projectile doesn't drop like a stone. In a vacuum it is even less likely to drop, why else would satellites continue to circle the earth even when the initial thrust has been removed?

What actually happens is that the turbulent air currents force the aircraft to drop or rise rapidly. In fact the height that we drop or rise appears to be greatly exaggerated. We have all experienced the feeling of thinking that we have reached the bottom step on a stairway to find that there is one more. The drop feels more like 3 feet than the actual 9 inches. Exactly the same applies with turbulence. We have been going along smoothly and when we start to buffet, each rise or fall is unexpected and has the same effect as the extra step. Once you learn to understand and to anticipate turbulence, it ceases to have that effect.

Air pockets cannot exist for more than a fraction of a second. When lightning occurs it creates a temporary vacuum. Thunder is the sound of air rushing to fill that vacuum. Similarly, when you crack a whip, the sound of the crack is the air rushing to fill the vacuum created by the lash. If for some meteorological reason an air pocket were to be created, it would close so quickly as to sound like thunder and even if the aircraft were to pass through it during the trillionth of a second that it existed, that aircraft wouldn't deviate one iota.

So, we can discount engine failure, wings falling off, turbulence and bad weather, but aren't most accidents attributable to:

HUMAN ERROR

14 Human error

I've no doubt that a powerful contributor to my fear of flying was the fact that I wasn't flying the plane myself. My fate was literally in the hands of several other people who were all complete strangers to me and one mistake by any of them could cost me my life. My experiences with the Eugines of this world didn't help any. At least in the car you can see where you are going and if it gets too hairy you are able to get out.

I believe Hollywood also helped to form my impression of the typical pilot: a fearless daredevil who has to be restrained from doing loop the loops. The Battle of Britain hero Douglas Bader lost his legs not through being shot down by the enemy, but because he was showing off by flying very low. Unfortunately, Douglas didn't allow for a margin of error.

Now that I know the actual character, quality and standard of professionalism of the modern commercial jet pilot, my cheeks blush when I think how incredibly arrogant and stupid I was ever to doubt them and I had every reason to know better.

Earlier I mentioned that I had applied to become a pilot during my two years' national service. In those days the vast majority of the cream of the country's youth chose the RAF rather than the army or navy and, in order to be considered for aircrew, you had to be a POM. No, not an affectionate Australian term for an Englishman, but Potential Officer Material.

Now, my general attitude was: I've got to waste two years of my life so I might just as well use it to do something useful by learning to fly. They'd warned us that a very high standard was necessary in order to be accepted, but I had no fears about that, I'd captained my school at rugby and cricket and was considered to be reasonably bright. After all, the RAF had invited us to apply, so they must have been anxious for pilots and I would do them a favour and become one.

The interview involved over 500 POMs spending a week at Hendon RAF camp, which was split into two parts. About 2 days were spending undergoing a medical, the like of which I hope never to be subjected to again. Bear in mind that we were young fit lads and had already passed a very strict medical in order to get into the RAF. Less than 20 per cent of the applicants passed the Hendon medical. I'm happy to say that I was one that did.

The rest of the week was spent doing application and co-ordination tests together with written tests. Out of the 500-plus applicants that week, not a single one was accepted for aircrew training. At the time I was rather piqued because they had failed to recognize a man that in all probability would have turned out to be the best pilot they had ever had. This is probably why the point that I am trying to make now didn't register then. You could be forgiven for thinking that the point was to blow my own trumpet. But you would be wrong. The point I'm making is, whether it be from the physical, mental or psychological aspect, whether we're talking about co-ordination, reflexes or intelligence, the man flying your plane is:

LA CRÈME DE LA CRÈME

In case you are worried that he might have a heart attack, sitting beside him is an equally competent specimen, the co-pilot. He is co-pilot, not because he is incapable – in fact he is experienced and perfectly capable of flying and landing the plane safely – but because he hasn't spent the required number of years to qualify as the chief pilot. In the trillion-to-one chance that the co-pilot should also have a heart attack, there is an ingenious system called auto-pilot. At the mere press of a button the aircraft will complete the flight and land safely.

For a moment, just put yourself in the place of the airlines. When I was in the RAF they would say: for every man in the air you need 1,000 dedicated people on the ground. An incredible amount of money is invested in those people, including the pilot. The aircraft itself costs several million pounds. No way are they going to entrust that massive investment to the flying equivalent of a Eugine or a fearless daredevil!

Occasionally you hear rumours of airlines cutting costs, either on cutting maintenance procedures or by using substandard parts. I'm not saying this has never happened, but it has never happened within "THE LIMITATIONS". Massive as the cost of a crash might be to an airline in loss of life and equipment, that loss would be insignificant compared to the loss of revenue if an airline had the reputation of being unsafe. It would mean certain bankruptcy.

The airlines recruit only experienced pilots who have obtained their experience either from military or civil flying or both. They are then retrained to fly one specific type of aircraft. Much of this training takes place in a simulator and the instructor ensures that anything that can go wrong, does go wrong, and always at the most critical time. Real-life emergencies are very rare, but if they do occur they seem rather routine compared to the experience that pilots accumulate in the simulator.

The airlines, and particularly the airlines within "THE LIMITATIONS", are indeed fortunate in that flying, rather like acting and the entertainment profession, is a highly sought-after profession. There are literally thousands of applicants for every top job available and they are able to select:

LA CRÈME DE LA CRÈME

They do not select fearless daredevils. Safety is the most important factor. They ensure that their pilots are not only conscious of the safety of their passengers, but of their own lives and those of the rest of the crew. If you feel frightened of just one flight, bear in mind that the pilot and the rest of the crew would not spend a large proportion of their lives flying through the air unless they knew that it was absolutely safe. They are not mindless and fearless idiots, they are highly intelligent and sensitive people who have no more desire to risk their own lives than they have to risk yours.

Perhaps Hollywood has also put into your mind that piloting is a very stressful job and that it is not uncommon for pilots to resort to alcohol or other drugs in order to cope with that stress. No, flying is only stressful to those who don't understand how safe it is; piloting is a highly responsible job, which isn't the same thing. The selection process ensures that only those who are equipped to carry the responsibility are chosen to take it.

There is probably no other profession that is subjected to the frequent physical and psychological medical check-ups that pilots have to go through. Strict regulations apply about the use of alcohol and other drugs. Pilots are highly paid, dedicated professionals. They love their job and there is no way they would risk losing their licence for a night out with the boys. Even if they did, there is no "omerta" in the flight cabin, unlike in the Mafia. If you break the code of silence in the Mafia, you risk your life. In the aviation game it is the complete opposite, you risk your life and that of your colleagues and your passengers if you don't say something.

If a member of the crew were to go astray, it would become obvious to his colleagues and, if they failed to notice it or to report it, they would be just as liable to lose their own jobs.

In civil aviation, safety takes precedence over everything else. And that's the way it should be.

Three of the questions in the big Q were:

1 Do you have a fear of driving?
2 Do you have a fear of being driven by some other drivers?
3 Do you have a fear of being driven by all other drivers?

89 per cent of the participants answered yes to question 2. Only 11 per cent had a fear when being driven by themselves but, surprisingly, 22 per cent had no fear of being driven by all other drivers. Why surprising? Because I'd formed the distinct impression when talking to sufferers of FOF that a major part of the problem was: not being in control. I'd always assumed that was the basic cause of my fear and that not being in control meant that I wasn't the pilot. I believe that the true feeling of not being in control, is not so much: I'm not the pilot, but: I don't understand or trust this whole situation.

If you watch golf on television you might have heard a commentator say:

"If your very life were to depend on sinking this putt, you couldn't have a better man to take it than..."

When flying, both you and the rest of the passengers are very fortunate that you are not flying the plane, so don't try to! Just sit back, relax and enjoy the flight. You are in no danger and one of the reasons is, the man who is in control is the flying equivalent of:

TIGER WOODS

OK, I take your point that the air crew wouldn't spend half their lives 35,000 ft above the earth unless they were

> convinced that it was safe, but what about the mechanics
> and the flight controllers? Their lives aren't on the line.

True, but they too are dedicated professionals. It is exactly because your life is in their hands that the same rigid standards are applied to their selection, training and supervision. Airplanes are serviced after every flight and are subjected to regular, meticulous inspections. Mechanics have to sign for work carried out and so does the supervisor. In addition all vital staff, both aircrew and ground staff, are subject to regular inspection by Transport Canada, which is completely independent of the airlines and gives no prior warning of such inspections.

Just put yourself in the position of a flight controller or a mechanic. You have hundreds of lives depending on you, to say nothing of your own reputation and career. Would you take the risk of allowing that plane to fly unless you were 100 per cent certain that it was mechanically sound, with the full knowledge that if a mechanical fault did occur, it would unerringly be traced back to you?

> I accept that they are proficient and dedicated, but they are
> also human and, no matter how dedicated they are, they
> can make a mistake. It only needs one mistake and I'm
> dead.

No it doesn't! Modern civil aviation has been described as very much a belt-and-suspender affair. The expression, though apt, is an understatement. Two belts and two pairs of suspenders would be more realistic. Of course it is human to err. Believe me, the airlines are more aware of this than you are. It is also true that, in the comparatively short history of aviation, many accidents can be attributed to human error. However, the main factor that makes modern civil aviation so incredibly safe is that after every one of those accidents, there is an inquest to determine its exact cause. Whether an accident is attributed to human error, mechanical failure, sabotage or to an unfortunate combination of several factors, the safety procedures are amended to ensure that, should that particular combination of events occur in the future, it will not result in a disaster.

A typical example is that on one occasion both pilots suffered from food poisoning because they selected the same meal, which turned out to be suspect. No accident resulted, but it is now standard procedure that pilots are forbidden to eat the same meal.

Pilots, engineers, mechanics and flight controllers are human and do make mistakes; this is why the procedures allow for this to ensure that, when they do, it will not result in disaster.

OK, you've convinced me that the plane won't fall out of the sky, that the wings won't fall off and that bad weather is no danger. I'm also convinced that the crew, mechanics and flight controllers are conscientious and competent and that, if they do make a mistake, the procedures have fail-safe systems to negate the error. But what about all these near misses I keep reading about; I've heard that the airways are now dangerously overcrowded and why are these flight controllers always on strike if it's not because they are overworked and under-paid? The wings might not fall off, but if we collide with another plane or fly into a mountain I'm still dead!

I can only agree with you. That was exactly the impression that I had and I've no doubt that it made a strong contribution to my fear of flying. So let's take a closer look at:

THE FLIGHT CONTROLLERS

15   The flight controllers

The media give the impression that flight controllers are always on strike. If they strike because they are overworked, or because the airways are dangerously overcrowded, then they have my support. Anything that makes flying even more safe than it already is has my support.

However, we need to get these crowded airways and near misses in proportion. From the moment your aircraft starts to taxi to the runway to the moment it completes taxiing at the destination airport, it is being observed on radar. On initial taxiing and take-off and landing and completion of taxiing it is also being physically observed by its own exclusive flight controller.

The sky is not one great open space through which aircraft can travel at whatever height or direction they choose. It is divided into specific airways, just like highways on land. There is, however, one very important difference. Whereas on highways, cars can hurtle along sometimes separated by only a few inches and, if there isn't a median, they regularly hurtle towards each other at closing speeds of 150 mph, the airplane has its own private motorway.

An aircraft flying at 35,000 ft is spaced so that the nearest aircraft either above or below it is 2,000 ft away. The nearest aircraft in front of, or behind it, is at least 10 miles away. Does that sound dangerous to you? Can you imagine how safe motoring would be if all cars were kept at least 10 miles apart? Air-traffic control not only ensures that you don't collide with other planes, but also that you don't fly into mountains or other obstructions.

So if that is the case, how come we have all these near misses, how come air collisions do actually occur and how come aircraft do actually fly into mountains?

This is where you need to keep things in proportion. We think a near miss is when aircraft fly within a few feet of each other. In fact a near miss is when two aircraft become closer than the stipulated distances laid down. As with every other aspect of flying, there is always a large safety margin. Mid-air collisions of flights included in "THE LIMITATIONS" are less than one in several billions. Aircraft do collide and fly into mountains. The event is so rare that, whether it is a private or military plane and no matter where in the world it happens, it still becomes headline news. That is probably the greatest tribute to the safety of flying generally. However, when you consider that those collisions invariably happen to military or private aircraft, what greater proof do you need of the incredible safety of the aircraft that fly within "THE LIMITATIONS"?

Now let's deal with other dangers that tend to be exaggerated by the media, beginning with:

HIJACKING AND SABOTAGE

16　Highjacking and sabotage

Ten years ago it seemed that aircraft were being hijacked and/or blown up every day. I don't think it helped when the appropriate authorities gave in to the initial hijackers. However, as with every other aspect where safety is involved, the civil-aviation industry has learned from experience. Saboteurs and hijackers tend to pick on a "soft touch" and civil aircraft have ceased to be a "soft touch".

Elaborate security screening systems for both passengers and baggage are now maintained at all airports within "THE LIMITATIONS". Some of the systems are obvious. Others are not and I felt reassured when the appropriate authorities refused to give me any details about them for obvious reasons.

The most important aspect about hijacking and sabotage is how rare they have become nowadays in the aviation industry. Even in the bad days the majority of such incidents were confined to flights outside "THE LIMITATIONS" and the vast majority of those incidents were successfully concluded without loss of life, or injury to passengers.

The notable exception was the Lockerbie disaster. During my research I asked hundreds of people: What was the last air disaster you can remember? A few couldn't remember any. The vast majority of those that did said Lockerbie. A few even said Munich. Lockerbie occurred over 10 years ago and Munich over 40 years ago. It is very unlikely that either disaster would have occurred if current safety and security systems were in operation.

Now let's dispel two other bogies than can cause concern to people who suffer from a fear of flying:

FOG AND FUEL

17   Fog and fuel

There's no doubt that in the early days fog did represent a hazard to flying. Today it has ceased to be a hazard. It can still be an inconvenience but even that is very rare. There are three main reasons for the improvement.

The first is acts that have abolished the burning of certain fossil fuels within "THE LIMITATIONS".

The second reason is the vast technical advances in both weather-forecasting and communications. If weather conditions could make the take-off hazardous, be it due to fog, ice or whatever, the plane will not take-off. If there are similar conditions prevailing at the destination airport, the plane will not take off.

But we all know that weather-forecasting is not an exact science and these flights can last several hours; what happens if the arrival airport becomes fog-bound during flight?

Before each flight a plan is prepared completely independent of the captain and crew. It will take into account the weather conditions, including the expected direction and strength of the winds and suggest the safest and most comfortable route. To the basic weight of the aircraft will be added the weight of the passengers and crew together with their baggage. From this information the amount of fuel required to complete the journey will be calculated and that calculation will also take into account the weight of the fuel.

As with every other aspect of aircraft safety, safety margins are added. If, for whatever reason, the plane cannot safely land at the planned destination, it will carry sufficient fuel to fly to an alternative pre-nominated airport and to circle over that airport for at least 30 minutes. To this total calculation is added a further safety margin to cover any possible contingency. The captain will check the flight plan and has authority to change it if he believes that it is hazardous in any way. By law he cannot take on less fuel than that shown by the flight plan. However, he can carry more fuel if he deems it necessary.

The third reason that fog has ceased to be a hazard today is that aircraft within "THE LIMITATIONS" have auto-pilot and can be beamed down perfectly safely, even if the visibility is zero! For airports that are equipped with "autoland", fog doesn't present a hazard to the landing itself, only to safe taxiing.

In my early days of motoring I would regularly run out of fuel, partly because I couldn't afford to put more than 2 gallons in at a time, but mainly because in those days cars didn't possess the warning systems that modern cars do. I know I'm tempting Sod's Law now, but I haven't run out for over 20 years.

By now you will know that the safety procedures on a modern civil aircraft make it impossible for it to run out of fuel whilst airborne. Even if a fuel leak were to arise, the quantity and consumption of fuel are checked throughout the flight and the moment that lack of fuel became a potential hazard, the plane would land at the nearest suitable airport to correct the leak and take on the extra fuel needed.

But supposing the plane develops a fuel leak in the middle of the Atlantic?

This is another myth. If you look at the most direct route between London and New York on a flat atlas, it looks as if you have to cross 3,000 miles of ocean. Look at the shortest route on a globe and it's via northern Europe and Canada. For noise abatement or environmental reasons you might appear to be flying mainly over water. In fact you are rarely far from the nearest airport. I've failed to find one single incident of aircraft within "THE LIMITATIONS" having to ditch in the sea!

Now, although completely natural, how can you possibly enjoy flying if you suffer from:

A FEAR OF HEIGHTS

18   A fear of heights

I still suffer from a fear of heights and I no longer have a fear of flying. Is that because I sit as far away from the windows as possible and block my mind from the fact that I'm 35,000 ft above the ground? On the contrary, I always prefer a window seat; even above the clouds, the scenery is more interesting than the interior of the aircraft. With a window seat you have the choice of either.

If it's a clear day a major part of the pleasure of flying is to be able to look at the scenery from a great height. We all enjoy a panoramic view. If you climb Everest, you'll only see the world from 29,000 ft and you'll be cold, exhausted and find it very difficult to breathe. Can you imagine the delights of observing a panoramic view of a range of snow-capped mountains from 35,000 ft, whilst sitting in shirtsleeves in an armchair, warm, relaxed, safe and comfortable?

But surely I'm contradicting myself. If I had a genuine fear of heights, there's no way that I could enjoy that view; on the contrary, I'd be petrified.

The answer to the conundrum is that no one has a fear of heights. What we all suffer from, or should suffer from if we are normal, is not a fear of heights, but a fear of falling from a height.

Let me give an example: Lake Titicaca is a huge lake and an area of great beauty and serenity. If you stood beside the lake, apart from the rarefied atmosphere, you would have no sensation of standing at a great height. In fact you would be standing 12,500 ft above sea level, higher than Mount Columbia, the highest mountain in Alberta. To use my own experience: if I entered a tall building and I was going up to, say, the 30th floor, in the lift I would be apprehensive of the ever-increasing gap between me and the ground floor. Once I stepped out of the lift I'd have no problem and be completely relaxed. However, if I walked over to a window and from 30 floors up could see nothing between me and the street below, the fear would return. It would be twice as bad if I had to walk out onto a balcony.

Apart from the fact that I am no longer apprehensive about lifts, the reason being that I know the lift cannot suddenly plunge to the ground, I still feel queasy near the window or on the balcony of a high building. This doesn't bother me. I'm aware that it is quite normal and part of my protection. I merely stay away from the windows and if I have to go on the balcony, I stand at the back of it.

I can go up a ladder without fear, providing:

I'm satisfied that the bottom is resting on firm ground at an angle such that it will not slide.

That the top is also resting against a solid surface that won't slip.

That I'm convinced that the rungs are firm and won't break.

That I can cling to the sides with both hands so that at any one time at least 3 of my limbs are in firm contact with the ladder.

It's the old belt-and-braces syndrome; provided I feel perfectly safe, I have no fear of heights. When I sit in an aeroplane nowadays, no matter what distance from the ground the plane is, I have no fear because I know that I'm perfectly safe.

From my own experiences and from talking to other

people who suffered from a fear of flying, I am convinced that just as a fear of heights isn't really a fear of heights but a fear of falling, so a fear of flying isn't really a fear of flying, but a fear that flying is dangerous and that once you satisfy yourself that there is no danger in flying, so the fear will go.

Perhaps the most significant question in the big Q was:

"Do you believe that your fear of flying would cease if you knew in advance that the plane would land safely?"

I fully expected the answer to be a unanimous yes. In fact 22 per cent of the participants answered no. I found this difficult to understand. I could have understood it if flying was like a hairy fairground ride. It surprised me that in the big Q, only 78 per cent had a fear of fairground rides. I was convinced it would be 100 per cent. But even if I knew that there was no danger, I'd still be fearful of an experience that separated my stomach from the rest of my body. But there's no way that you could compare flying in a modern jet with a fairground ride. Even on the short and rare occasions that you do experience turbulence, it is no worse than driving over cobblestones.

So I contacted each one of them and asked them to explain to me how they could possibly have a fear of flying if they knew in advance that they would arrive safely. Most of them were unable to give a coherent explanation. One of them said: "It's just the thought of that vast space between me and the ground."

I could relate to that. This is why I still feel apprehensive when standing on the edge of the balcony of a tall building. Even so, I have no fear of height when sitting 35,000 ft above the earth in a jet plane. I think the key was in a hot-air-balloon flight that Joyce and I took over Carson Valley in Nevada.

It was during the time when I had lost my fear of flying but was still apprehensive. When I had my fear of flying there is no way that you could have induced me to go up in a hot-air balloon. You still couldn't induce me to go on a hairy fairground ride. I had a feeling of excitement both before and during the balloon trip. At one time we reached 5,000 ft and the pilot turned off the hot air. I suffered fear of neither height nor danger. In fact it was one of the most exhilarating experiences of my life.

Why did I have no fear of falling from 5,000 ft when I still have fear of standing on the edge of a balcony at 30 ft? Because the edge of the basket was the height of my chest, and like the ladder, I could cling on to the basket with both hands and there was no way I could fall out of that basket. But the basket was 5,000 ft up. Supposing the balloon had suddenly plunged to the ground. There was no way that the balloon could suddenly plunge to the ground. It was full of hot air and the basket was firmly attached to the balloon.

There was no sense of fear because I knew there was no danger. On a balcony where the guard comes up to my waist, I could slip and topple over. Or perhaps the construction engineer has miscalculated the weight that the balcony can take. Or perhaps the "cowboys" who built it used defective materials. So I might just as well move back and feel safe.

Let me put it to you another way. The earth moves on its axis every 24 hours and the circumference is approximately 25,000 miles. So, standing on the circumference, we are spinning at a speed of over a thousand miles an hour. At the same time we encircle the sun every 365 days, or every 8,760 hours. I'm informed that the sun is 92 million miles from the earth and, if my mathematics teacher earned his salary, that means we travel nearly 600 million miles through space every 8,760 hours, which is a speed of nearly 70,000 miles per hour.

As you sit in your garden on a lovely summer's day, gently rocking backwards and forwards in your swing-chair, are you conscious of the fact that you are hurtling through space at nearly 70,000 miles per hour and at the same time spinning at over 1,000 miles per hour? Are you conscious of the incredible vastness of the space surrounding this earth? However, if the earth stopped spinning and you were shot off into space at 1,000 mph, or if the earth suddenly stopped moving round the sun and you were shot off at 70,000 mph, you would become very conscious of it.

So why do we get no impression of these incredible speeds when sitting in our garden? Because the garden and atmosphere above it are moving and spinning in the same directions at the same speed. In a sense we are cocooned in our own little world and because we don't worry about the earth stopping spinning or moving, we have no fear. That's how I felt during the balloon ride. I knew there was no danger and therefore there was no fear, not even of height. I was cocooned in the little world of the balloon basket and therefore effectively standing on the ground. Without the fear of height, the panoramic views were a joy to behold and the gentle movements of the balloon, whether they were up or down, sideways or forwards, were equivalent to the gentle rocking of the swing-chair.

Once you lose the fear, a flight in a modern jet is exactly the same; at 35,000 ft there is no sensation of speed. You are cocooned in a little world of your own and it's a nice, comfortable, relaxed world. You have your own comfortable armchair, the temperature is controlled to suit you. You are breathing clean fresh air of a quality you won't enjoy once you leave the aircraft. You have attractive and cheerful stewards and stewardesses to serve you drinks and meals. Rather like hospital food, airline meals have become the butt of comedians' jokes. I agree that some years ago the reputation was justified. However, the civil-aviation industry is highly competitive and in recent years, just as incredible advances have been made in your and their No. 1 priority – safety, so have similar advances been made in the second priority: your pleasure and comfort. Personally I find the average meal served nowadays by the airlines within

"THE LIMITATIONS" to be both nutritious and edible.

I can understand someone thinking: "Even if I knew the plane would land safely, I still couldn't get over that fear of all the space between me at 35,000 ft and the ground." Once you are in the cocoon, you are not effectively 35,000 ft above the ground, you are merely sitting on the ground in a comfortable armchair. When you have a fear of flying, it is hard to believe that for most of the flight you are not even aware that you are flying. You can quite happily eat, sleep or read a book, in perfect comfort.

Now, the reason that you don't fear that the earth will stop, is because the possibility of it happening is so remote as not to worry you. It's exactly the same when flying within "THE LIMITATIONS". The chances of something bad happening are so remote that you have no need to worry about them!

Possibly you are saying:

"Yes I know that, but that billion-to-one chance could happen to me and with my luck it will happen to me!"

Then you are being incredibly stupid. If you worry that the one plane that you are travelling in will crash, why aren't you worried that the thousands of other planes that fly over you every day of your life won't fall out of the sky and land on you? Do you duck every time you hear a plane go overhead? Of course you don't, because you know that planes don't just fall out of the sky.

Earlier I said that you won't need to use courage. Do you need courage to get on a train? In the big Q the only form of transport that not one single participant had a fear of was travel by train. Why was that? Because we regard travel by train as both normal and safe.

What I do need you to do is to think positively. You are reading this book because you know that the fear that prevents you from flying, or makes it such a horrendous experience when you do, is not a very pleasant thing to have. At the same time you also know that flying, within "THE LIMITATIONS" is the safest form of transport and that your fears are illogical.

I want you first to accept that death is inevitable. Sooner or later you are going to die. Even if you spent the whole of your life flying at 35,000 ft in aircraft within "THE LIMITATIONS", the odds are less than one in a million against flying being the cause of your death.

So, stop torturing yourself unnecessarily. You don't like being someone who is afraid of flying. It makes you feel irrational, illogical and insecure. You have it within your power, not only to take your first or next flight as the case might be, but actually to enjoy it. Life isn't meant to be just a mere existence. Life is meant to be lived to the full.

Your fifth instruction is:

GO FOR IT!

Accept that you are going to take that first or next flight whether you like it or not. Now, from this point on, the time prior to the flight, the flight itself and your future life can either be a nightmare or an enjoyable and fulfilling experience.

You might feel that this depends upon kismet. No it doesn't, it depends entirely upon you. The pessimist sees the bottle as half empty and the optimist sees it as half full. These are two different ways of perceiving the same situation. If you fear a flight within "THE LIMITATIONS", you are perceiving a bottle that is actually full as empty.

It is entirely within your control. The fact is that it will be a very pleasant and safe experience. You have the choice of looking forward to the exciting and exhilarating experience that it actually will be, or you can distort the true situation and turn it into a nightmare. The choice is yours. Either way you are still going to take that flight. Are you going to make it nightmare or exhilaration? Stupid question. Your sixth instruction is, not only are you going to take that first or next flight, but you are going to look forward to it and:

ENJOY IT!

Since I discovered the easy way to stop smoking, I have claimed that it is easy to solve any problem that is mainly mental, whether it be weight loss, alcohol, other chemical addictions, or changing anything else in your life that causes you suffering. It is easy provided you follow the instructions. It is easy, but don't underrate yourself. All creatures on this planet can swim naturally. It is only the human being that, because of the brainwashing we receive from birth, has to learn to swim. That fact doesn't lessen the joy every human being feels when they complete those first strokes, or the first width, or learn to ride a bicycle, or pass their driving test.

You are about to achieve something marvellous; both anticipate and luxuriate in the feeling that you are about to solve this debilitating problem. And do it now! All the instructions are important, but the sixth instruction is the nicest:

ENJOY IT!

Now, I'm aware that you might still have reservations and that I still haven't dealt with some factors that can add to the fear of flying. The point I want to get home to you is that many of these other factors do not cause the fear of flying, but only appear to be relevant because we have a fear of flying, and that once we have removed the fear of flying they cease to be relevant. Possibly the worst of these feelings is:

CLAUSTROPHOBIA

19 Claustrophobia

My *Oxford Everyday Dictionary* defines claustrophobia as:

An abnormal fear of being in an enclosed space.

As I stated earlier, my wife Joyce suffers from claustrophobia; I
never have. On the contrary, when I was a child it caused some
consternation to my parents when they entered my bedroom
in the morning, to discover my feet on the pillow and my head
buried beneath the blankets at the bottom of the bed.

I can remember that it didn't bother me, but for the life
of me I cannot remember why. I can only surmise that it was
because I was more afraid of the dark or the ghosts that I might
see and, more important, who might see me if my head
remained on the pillow.

It wasn't until I started to research the fear of flying that
it occurred to me that Joyce's claustrophobia only appeared to
surface when she was about to enter an elevator. Now, I've
never suffered from claustrophobia, but I have suffered from a
fear of elevators or, more accurately, certain elevators.
Moreover, people who believe they suffer from claustrophobia
will usually quote their fear of elevators as a classic example.

The downstairs cloakroom is the smallest room in our
house. I asked Joyce if she ever got claustrophobia when using
it. The answer was an emphatic no. I pointed out that it was
half the size of the average elevator, so why did she get
claustrophobia in the elevator but not in the cloakroom?

We discussed the subject at some length. She eventually

came to the conclusion that the cause of her claustrophobia was not the confined space itself, but a combination of three factors:

1 In an elevator, there is a fear of height, in case the elevator falls.
2 In an elevator, if the elevator breaks down between floors, you are not in control, you are trapped.
3 Genuine claustrophobia. If the elevator does break down, you are in a confined space, the supply of oxygen can be exhausted and, if it is, you will suffocate.

So, like a fear of flying, claustrophobia would appear to be more complicated than simply an abnormal fear of confined spaces. In fact, as in Joyce's case, the confined space had nothing to do with it and I suspect this is true of the vast majority of people who believe they suffer from claustrophobia.

Her fear of elevators was really a combination of three fears:

Falling from a great height
Being trapped
Suffocation

You could possibly add two other fears if the elevator failure was caused by a power cut: the fear of the dark, and the fear of fire. Who knows what proportion each of these fears contributes to an overall fear of elevators? In my case there was no confusion: it was purely a fear that the cable connected to the counter-weight might snap and I'd go plunging to the ground. That particular point never worried Joyce. In her case it was a combination of being trapped and not being able to breathe.

I would also contend that if you have genuine reason to believe that you might be subjected to any of the above fears when entering an elevator, then your fear of elevators is neither abnormal nor a phobia. On the contrary it is not only normal but rational.

I no longer have a fear of elevators. I'm not saying that I get the same feeling of excitement and exhilaration that I do from flying, but that's because a ride in an elevator is a pretty mundane experience. However, I really appreciate being able to experience a ride in an elevator with boredom rather than fear. In fact the only thing I dislike about elevator rides nowadays is the embarrassment when every occupant stands staring at the doors in complete silence, desperately trying to avoid eye contact with their fellow occupants.

Why did I lose my fear of elevators? Was it because I stopped being a jellyfish and applied positive thinking? No, my fear of elevators was because I believed that if the chain snapped, I'd go hurtling to the ground. If the elevator was crowded, I'd find that little plaque that told you the maximum number of passengers. I'd count the number of passengers. I would weigh every one of those passengers in my mind. In the US it was a particularly frightening experience. Half the population seemed to be grossly overweight, and it was always that half that crammed into the elevator that I was using. Had the elevator manufacturer allowed for such eventualities?

I lost my fear of elevators because I now know that even if all the passengers were overweight and it were possible to cram three times as many of them into the elevator, that elevator still couldn't plunge to the ground. I found out that there wasn't just one steel cable which connected the elevator to the counter-weight but six to eight and that just one of those cables was strong enough to hold the elevator with a full complement of occupants. Even in the impossible event of all the cables breaking at the same time, elevators are also equipped with an automatic braking system.

Just like the civil-aviation industry, elevator manufacturers apply the belt-and-suspenders principle. I now know the elevator cannot fall and therefore, even in the elevator of a hundred-storey skyscraper, the gap beneath the elevator is completely irrelevant, so I no longer have to torture myself by thinking about it. I'm cocooned in my safe little world.

I also know that if the elevator did break down, even if it were overcrowded, and no matter how long we had to wait, there would be an ample supply of air and we wouldn't suffocate. In reality all modern elevators have an alarm button, and the vast majority have a telephone. On the comparatively rare occasions that an elevator does break down, in the vast majority of them, rescue rarely takes longer than a few minutes.

Be honest, have you ever heard of a single case of an elevator plunging to the ground? Try asking other people, see if you can find someone that even knows someone that hurtled to the ground in an elevator. It cannot happen. So why do we worry about it? Because we've all seen it happen many times in films. We've been brainwashed. We need to remove the brainwashing.

I've been saying that we all know that flying is the safest form of transport. In fact it isn't. It is incredibly safe, many times more so than cars, buses, coaches and even trains. In fact the safest form of transport is elevators. In the big Q I was surprised that only 22 per cent suffered from claustrophobia. I thought it would be more. 33 per cent had a fear of elevators. Again I was surprised that it wasn't larger.

However, for me, the most surprising revelation from the big Q was that not one participant had a fear of travelling in trains. I have no fear whatsoever of flying within "THE LIMITATIONS" but I still confess to an apprehension about trains. Flying within "THE LIMITATIONS" is safer than trains.

Only 11 per cent expressed a fear of escalators. Elevators are even safer than escalators. No one dies from riding on an escalator. You might argue that in the King's Cross disaster, many people died from riding on an escalator. I would argue that it was not the escalator that killed them but the fact that it caught fire and that it was fire or smoke inhalation that killed them. However, it's a moot point and I'll concede the point to you if you insist.

People don't die in elevators because they suffocate or hurtle to the ground. There are many more serious accidents on escalators than there are in elevators. If you do have a fear of elevators, I want you to remove it first because you are not likely to remove your fear of flying whilst you still suffer from a fear of elevators. Do not start with one of those transparent elevators on the outside of a high building. Why not, aren't they as safe as internal elevators? I'm sure they are, but remember that a fear of heights is quite normal. It's a natural instinct that we are trying to overcome. It's just like a balcony on a high building.

Look at it this way. Imagine you were riding in an internal elevator and one of your fellow passengers stood there saying:

> "Hey! We're 30 floors up. That's 300 ft! Can you imagine what will happen to us if this thing falls?"

He'd be reinforcing the brainwashing that we have been subjected to by Hollywood. Our whole object is to remove that brainwashing. The elevator cannot fall, but he would be trying to persuade us that it could. The point is that he would be reminding us of the height. That is exactly what those transparent, external elevators do. I can ride them today, but they make me feel uncomfortable. The people who design them are fools. When I go up in an elevator I don't do it for kicks. If I needed kicks I'd go on a fairground ride. I hate fairground rides. When I use an elevator I want to feel safe and comfortable, and by making sure that I'm constantly aware of the height, the stupid idiots are achieving the exact opposite to what they should want to achieve:

THEY ARE PUSHING ME TO THE EDGE OF THE BALCONY!

If you suffer from a fear of elevators, or are somewhat apprehensive about them, I want you to take that elevator ride, not with a feeling of doom and gloom, but with a feeling of excitement and exhilaration. I know I've said there is nothing particularly exciting or exhilarating about a ride in an elevator. But for you there is. The mere fact that you'll be able to take advantage of the convenience of riding in elevators for the rest of your life, without feeling apprehensive, will be sufficient reward in itself. But you'll have an even greater bonus. When you have removed your fear of elevators, you'll know that you'll also be able to remove your fear of flying.

Don't wait until the next time you have to go up in an elevator. Go to a hotel or shopping mall or whatever, just for the joy of proving that you can do it. Don't just do one trip. Go up and down as high and as often as you want to:

GO FOR IT!

Now let's reconsider:

MY FIRST FLIGHT

20 My first flight

Why was my first flight so horrendous? For exactly the same reason that my earlier experiences of being driven by Eugine were such a nightmare: because in both cases I was convinced that my life was in danger. In the case of Eugine:

I WAS ABSOLUTELY RIGHT!

And my one regret is that I didn't have the sense or courage to admit my fear and take the train, or perhaps I was too sensitive to tell him or lacked the confidence to tell him. Perhaps my fear of appearing to be a coward in the eyes of my wife and colleagues was greater than my fear of Eugine's driving. Maybe that, just as 56 per cent of the participants in the big Q felt their fear of flying was irrational, I felt my fear of Eugine's driving was irrational. Who can tell?

I certainly couldn't at the time and reviewing the situation over 40 years later I'm not much wiser. As I've said: it's the confusion that causes the problem and I've no doubt that all of the factors that I have mentioned came into the equation. All that I can tell you is that, when a similar episode occurred years later, there was no confusion, and should a similar experience occur in the future, there would be no confusion. I'd get my priorities right and put my life and safety first even if it meant offending the driver.

My first flight was many times more horrendous than Eugine's driving, but in that case:

I WAS ABSOLUTELY WRONG!

The confusion was even greater because I knew that Eugine's driving was dangerous and that flying was safe. So my feelings of cowardice and fear appeared to be even more irrational. The point is that because I didn't understand the true facts about flying:

I DIDN'T REALLY BELIEVE THAT IT WAS SAFE

Therefore I was neither being cowardly, nor was I being irrational; if you believe that flying is dangerous, it is quite rational that you should fear it.

It is significant that in the big Q that only 22 per cent of participants had a fear of being driven by all other drivers, that 11 per cent had a fear of driving when being driven by themselves and 89 per cent had a fear of being driven by some other drivers.

Isn't this the key to the whole affair! When being driven by a Eugine the whole journey *is* a nightmare. And it's not only Eugine's driving that worries you, you're now worried that every other driver on the road is a Eugine. I've no doubt that the most dangerous, and yet still the most common, fault that the Eugines of this world possess is tail-gating, or driving at 70 mph in the outside lane, up the backside of Eugine 2, who refuses to move over. It matters not that the inside and the middle lanes are completely free. Eugine 2 is travelling at the maximum speed limit so he knows that right is on his side and it doesn't matter how often Eugine 1 hoots and flashes his lights, Eugine 2 won't move over.

The true reason that he won't move over isn't because he is a respectful and conscientious bastion of civilization, and not only doesn't want to break the law himself, but feels it's his duty to make sure that Eugine 1 doesn't break it either, but because he already has two endorsements for speeding and will lose his licence if he gets another. Quite apart from that, he's driving the latest supercharged sports car, and if he hadn't got those endorsements, he'd show Eugine 1 who's the fastest gun on the motorway.

However, Eugine 1 isn't so easily thwarted. He decides to prove that he is in fact even more stupid than Eugine 2 by overtaking on the inside. When he does so, 1 and 2 are so intent on flashing, hooting, glaring, shouting and making obscene signs to each other, neither of them notice that, at the exact moment number 2 decides to overtake on the inside, Eugine 3, who has a faster car than either of them, has quickly sized up the situation and is already overtaking both of them on the inside.

Whenever driving conditions are wet or icy or visibility is badly impaired, there are always multiple pile-ups. You wonder how that can possibly happen. After all, most drivers understand the principles and will pull up safely if there is a pile-up. Most likely the driver behind will also stop safely. The trouble is, it only needs the occasional Eugine in the chain and he'll send those previous cars crashing into the cars in front.

When I watch the Eugines, I find the mystery to be not why there are so many pile-ups, but why there are so few. Politely ask them if they don't think it's rather dangerous to be travelling at 80 miles per hour just 2 yards behind another car and they'll justify it by explaining what incredibly fast reactions they have and how their car can pull up quicker than the car in front. Unfortunately they are often quite correct. Then try to explain to them that, no matter how quick their reactions or how efficient their vehicle's braking system is, they will already have ploughed into the back of the other car before they even realize it is braking. Some of the Eugines of this world do possess incredibly quick reactions. However, all of them are incredibly thick and unfortunately their quick reactions do not compensate for their stupidity.

Another mystery about Eugines is why they are so

intolerant of each other. You sit there shaking at the knees every time a Eugine jumps the lights 5 seconds after it has changed to red, or does a Grand Prix start the split second they change to orange. On both occasions you close your eyes and pray that Eugine 2 doesn't do his Grand Prix start while No. 1 is crossing the lights, or vice versa. When they do have a near miss or pile into each other, do they say: "So you jumped the lights, don't worry, I always do that and perhaps I was partly to blame by jumping the gun." Have you once in your life seen one of them do that? No way! They just start shouting and waving fists at each other.

Have you also noticed how Eugines, in spite of the fact that they regularly, deliberately and repeatedly break the law, risking their own lives and those of their passengers, pedestrians and fellow road-users, are so intolerant of any road-user that makes an unintentional error? To them their right of way is sacrosanct. At the same time they refuse to recognize that other road-users have any right of way. You often see them actually speed up on a roundabout to prevent some other driver from entering it safely. I think it should be compulsory for every Eugine to have engraved on his tombstone: Here lies Eugine, a man of principle. His dying words were:

I HAD RIGHT OF WAY!

Perhaps I might appear to have wandered from the point. I promise you that I haven't. If you are being driven by a good driver, the countless Eugines on the road will present little threat to you. You know that your driver will recognize them, anticipate them and avoid the shenanigans of getting involved with them. In other words you can relax and enjoy the journey.

However, if you are being driven by a Eugine, you know that far from avoiding his fellow Eugines, and much as he hates them, he just won't be able to resist them. Sometimes a whole line of them will be doing the conga, nose to tail in the outside lane all because the leading Eugine with the endorsements won't move over.

Apart from tail-gating, I think the second most common fault on motorways is when you come up to overtake a car in the centre lane which is about to overtake a truck also in the centre lane. Just as you are about to overtake that car, it signals to move out. In the vast majority of cases it's just an over-careful driver who wants to give plenty of warning that he wishes to overtake the truck once you have passed.

However, occasionally it is either a lapse of concentration by a careful driver or a Eugine who is going to move out anyway because he has right of way. A good driver will make sure it's neither before he overtakes. A Eugine will overtake regardless. The result is often two less Eugines on the roads, which I have no complaints about. But all too often they also kill their passengers and a careful driver who just happened to make a mistake when a Eugine was overtaking.

When you are being driven by a Eugine you can't relax even if you try to. You know that there are many other Eugines on the road. Some of them are so Euginic that even your own Eugine cannot fail to recognize them and realize that he is out-gunned. But some of them are geniuses of disguise. You cannot relax for a moment and the fact that you are not driving the car just makes it worse. Your life is in the hands of the "thicko" sitting beside you.

When the doors of that airplane slammed shut, it was like the doors of a prison slamming shut. The feeling of claustrophobia or of feeling trapped that I felt had in fact nothing to do with claustrophobia or of feeling imprisoned. The animal-rights activists have quite rightly brought attention to the conditions that calves are subjected to in order to sustain the veal trade. Anyone who has regularly travelled on London tube trains in the rush hour during a heat-wave would envy those calves. But for years I suffered the obvious and real lack of oxygen. When the doors closed, I had no means of opening them, but I didn't feel trapped. Even when the train was held up in a tunnel, which seemed hardly wider than the train itself, for half an hour, the heat and shortage of oxygen were even more apparent and real and there was still no feeling of being trapped.

I can't pretend that it was an exciting or exhilarating experience. It was decidedly unpleasant. But there was no element of fear because there was no feeling of danger. However, had I been in a similar position the day following the King's Cross fire, I've no doubt that I would have been not only uncomfortable but very frightened. I'd love to know how many people booked a transatlantic passage the day after they watched *Titanic* or how many swam in the ocean the day after watching *Jaws*. We'll never know but I can guarantee that I wouldn't have been one of them.

No matter how unpleasant the London tube is during the rush hour in a heat-wave, I would have undergone the experience every day of the year rather than suffer the horror of that first flight. Sufferers from a fear of flying complain about a feeling of claustrophobia, of being trapped, of not being in control and many other things. Yet 100 per cent have no fear of getting on trains and I'm not now talking about London tube trains but what was until recently British Rail. The space of a large modern jet-liner is no more confined. You are just as trapped on the train. True, you can open the door, but once you've started you can't get off until the train stops.

True, you can pull the emergency handle but have you ever done so? Of course not. Unless there's a genuine emergency, why would you even want to pull the handle? Why would you want to get off? After all, you got on that train for a specific purpose – to get from A to B – and you've paid a considerable sum for the privilege. Why on earth would you want to get off before you arrived at B?

I can suggest only one valid reason: that you were petrified that the train was unsafe, and had no desire to get on it in the first place.

Once you realize that flying is absolutely safe, these secondary aggravations, like claustrophobia, panic attacks, feeling trapped, not feeling in control, miraculously disappear with the fear and you begin to see flying as it really is:

AN EXHILARATING, EXCITING EXPERIENCE

BUT:
DON'T TRY TO FLY THE PLANE

21 Don't try to fly the plane

When a good driver is at the wheel, the passengers can relax, enjoy the scenery and the journey. If a Eugine is driving, there is no way that you can relax and you don't even see the scenery. In fact you daren't take your eyes off the road. Effectively you are driving the car.

Eugine's real ambition is to be a Grand Prix driver. However, he also has a secret desire to be a tour guide and finds no difficulty in combining his two loves at one and the same time. He is such a capable driver and his reactions are so quick that he finds no problem in taking his eyes off the road. In fact he gives the distinct impression that his car is equipped with auto-pilot as he gives a running commentary whilst he points out every boring feature of the landscape. So good a driver is he that he can judge to within 6 inches as he drifts towards the ditch and is completely unperturbed by the horns of the oncoming traffic as he drifts over the centre white line.

It's exactly the same when you suffer from a fear of flying. You find yourself not only trying to pilot the plane, but taking over the duties of the navigator and – in particular – the flight engineer. I'll refer to this situation as "Trying to Fly the Plane".

I have described how other books tended to concentrate on describing detailed techniques on how to cope with panic attacks and other physical symptoms caused by fear of flying and that the key to my method is that, by first removing the fear, you also remove the unpleasant physical effects and have no need to waste your time learning how to cope with them. Similarly the other books go into great detail about everything that happens during the flight, from entering the departure airport to leaving the destination airport.

Now, I agree that a brief explanation of certain aspects of the flight is not only helpful but essential; however, I also believe that too detailed an explanation of certain matters can be counter-productive and encourages the tendency of "Trying to Fly the Plane".

Probably the best way to illustrate the point is to compare that first horrendous experience with:

MY LAST FLIGHT

22 My last flight

Should you find the title of this chapter somewhat ambiguous and think it means that I will never fly again, I should explain that the comparison is between my first flight and my most recent flight, or, for that matter, any of the many flights I have experienced since my apprehension about flying became a joy of flying.

I should also point out that I have used some poetic licence in the comparison. By that, I do not mean that I have deliberately exaggerated either the horror of the first flight or the joy of the last. What I mean is that I'm not just trying to illustrate the difference between my first and latest flights, but the difference between a flight when you suffer from FOF and are "Trying to Fly the Plane" and a flight when you don't suffer from FOF and can just sit back, relax, trust the crew to fly the plane, and enjoy yourself.

For example: there were no hijacking or bomb scares when I took that first flight. I've therefore used my imagination to describe what effect it would have had on me in those days. I've also incorporated experiences expressed to me by other sufferers of FOF, which hadn't occurred to me, as if they were my own. My intention is not to distort or deceive; if it were, I wouldn't even mention the poetic licence. My intention is merely to illustrate how, once you remove the fear, the same experience can change from a nightmare to a pleasure.

The first thing to get into your mind is that the most important thing is not your first or next flight, whichever it happens to be, but the achievement of your goal. Try to imagine the exhilaration of Olympic gold-medal winners as they stand on the rostrum, heads held high, unashamed tears rolling down their cheeks, proudly watching their country's flag being hoisted to the tune of its national anthem. That might be the most exhilarating moment in their lives because it was the culmination of years of hard work and intensive training.

But the most important moment was when they decided to achieve that dream. Because unless they had experienced that moment they would never have achieved their goal. The most important moment for you was when you decided to do something about your fear of flying. Now, the Olympic athlete cannot achieve his or her goal without years of arduous preparation, training and discipline. Arduous it might be, but do you not feel they enjoy the challenge?

Fortunately for you, there is no need to go through years of arduous training; all you have to do is to follow the instructions and you can not only enjoy the achievement itself, but also the preparation. You possess one other even greater advantage over a potential Olympic gold-medal winner: a thousand athletes might have been equally motivated to win a particular event but only one of them can win the gold medal, whereas there is no limit to the number of people who can enjoy flying within "THE LIMITATIONS" and any sufferer from FOF can achieve that goal, provided:

THEY FOLLOW ALL THE INSTRUCTIONS

That was your first instruction. Your third was to:

START OFF IN A HAPPY FRAME OF MIND

Your fourth was to:

THINK POSITIVELY

Your fifth was to:

GO FOR IT!

And your sixth was:

ENJOY IT!

Now you are possibly wondering about two things:

1 Why do I treat you like an imbecile by repeating instructions which were blatantly obvious in the first place? And:
2 Why did I fail to repeat the second instruction?

Do you remember what the second instruction was? If you've forgotten, you now know why I needed to remind you of the other four. Even if I malign you and you have remembered them, or noted them down, I make no apologies. The reason that I remind you is that you need to be constantly aware of them and if you are now curious as to what the second instruction was, there is no need to start referring back. All the instructions are listed in Appendix B, together with the appropriate page number.

The preparation for your next flight doesn't start when you arrive at the departure airport. It has already started and the important time is:

NOW!

On my first flight I was obsessed with negative thoughts. I used my imagination to torture myself by worrying about all the things that could possibly go wrong and the worst one was: would I have the courage to get on that plane?

I would try not to think about it. That was the worst mistake of all. It's like when you have a big day coming up and get to bed an hour earlier because it's essential that you get a good night's sleep. It's Sod's Law again: not only do you lie awake the entire night, tossing and turning, but the more you worry about it, the more you guarantee that you won't be able to sleep. That is your seventh instruction:

DO NOT TRY TO TAKE YOUR MIND OFF THE FLIGHT

It is impossible to do that anyway, and if you try you will merely create a phobia. But the important point is: there is no need to take your mind off it. There is nothing bad happening, on the contrary:

THERE IS SOMETHING MARVELLOUS HAPPENING!!!

It might be impossible to take your mind off a particular subject, but what you are able to do is to have pleasant, positive thoughts rather than frightening, negative thoughts. Believe me: you have the choice. You are going to "Go For It". Whether you like it or not, you are going to take that next flight. You have the simple choice of making the time leading up to it a misery and, if you do, in all probability the flight itself will be a misery, or you can make that preparation time a pleasant anticipation of achieving your goal and, if you do, I guarantee that the flight itself will be both a doddle and a pleasure.

So what thoughts went through my mind during the time preceding my last flight? I no longer think about the flight itself. Just think: people pay thousands of dollars to spend holidays on ocean liners. Travel in any form can be exhilarating and entertaining, providing you are not in fear of your life. Only 44 per cent of the participants of the big Q had a fear of boats. But even the largest and safest of luxury liners are less safe than aircraft within "THE LIMITATIONS". Turbulence at sea is far greater than you'll experience in the air. I've only ever been on two cruises. On one of them half the passengers were sea-sick for 3 days. I've got a particularly queasy stomach, but during the hundreds of flights that I have now undertaken, I've never felt the slightest bit sick nor known of another passenger being sick.

So, whereas the cruise itself tends to be the holiday, I choose flying as the cheapest, quickest and safest means to travel relatively long distances, whether it be for business or pleasure. To say that I regard each flight as an exhilarating experience would not be true. I can only compare it to going to a holiday location by car or train.

On my first flight both the anticipation and the flight were horrendous and the holiday itself was ruined because of my fear of the return flight. During the period when the fear had turned to apprehension, I wasn't happy until the plane had landed safely and the holiday didn't start until that point. During the period of the holiday, I would have occasions when I would be thinking about the return flight with apprehension, but those thoughts didn't dominate or ruin my holiday.

Nowadays if I'm going on holiday by air, I enjoy thinking about and anticipating that holiday; the fact that I am flying no longer bothers me. On the day of the holiday, even if I have to get up in the middle of the night to catch the plane, I'm exhilarated. I'm already on holiday. The drive to the airport, the flight itself are all part of that excitement because there is no fear. Any sad thoughts during the holiday are not because I've got to fly home, but because the holiday is coming to an end.

A more relevant comparison is not a comparison of my last flight, but of the first flight I took after I'd lost my fear of flying. I would emphasize that I'd already lost my fear of flying before I took that flight. Again you might feel that there is a chicken-and-egg situation: how could I know that I'd actually lost my fear or apprehension at that stage, until I had taken the flight and proved it?

I could equally argue: how could I have possibly known that I would have a fear of flying until I'd actually experienced my very first flight? The answer to each paradox is the same: I didn't need actually to experience my first flight in order to possess a fear of flying; society had brainwashed me with misconceptions which made me believe that flying was dangerous. My fear of flying was natural. Once these misconceptions had been removed, so had my fear of flying, which is why, as Adelle describes in her introduction, the fear having already been removed, she couldn't wait to prove it. Neither could I.

The next flight I took was the second most exhilarating experience in my life. (The first was when it dawned on me that I had actually escaped from the nicotine prison.) It was exhilarating, not because it was part of a pleasant holiday, but because it was the proof of what I already knew:

MY FEAR OF FLYING WAS GONE FOR EVER!

Now what I want you to think about from now on isn't:

"Won't it be lovely if I can find the courage to fly so that I can enjoy a holiday with my family and friends or accompany my partner on a business trip." But:

"The holiday or business trip aren't important. The important thing is that I'm going to shed the shackles of being afraid to fly. I'm going to escape from this prison!"

Just like the Olympic gold-medal winner, whose exhilaration comes from achieving that goal, your exhilaration will be in achieving your goal:

TO BE ABLE TO FLY WITHOUT FEAR!

Between now and the actual flight, keep a happy and positive frame of mind. Don't worry that you keep thinking about it. It's what you are actually thinking that is important. Remember you have the choice and this is your eighth instruction: from now on:

YOU ARE GOING TO TAKE CONTROL

Flying is incredibly safe – that is a fact. So if between now and the actual flight you find yourself thinking about it:

THINK POSITIVELY!

Don't torture yourself with thoughts of what can go wrong. Instead remind yourself of how incredibly safe it is to fly. In particular look forward to the pleasure of achieving your goal. Picture yourself sitting there calm and relaxed and completely in control. Picture yourself looking around the other passengers, recognizing the ones that are going through the same traumas that you used to and feeling sympathy for them.

I once had the honour of chauffeuring my best friend and his shy young daughter to her wedding. She was in a state verging on panic, worrying about her dress, her hair and all the other things that brides worry about. I pulled the car over and stopped. Initially this just made the situation worse because we were already late and she began to remonstrate with me.

I told her to shut up. This took some courage on my part because at that moment in time my role was more chauffeur than friend. I pointed out that for the bride to be late was not only forgivable, but an essential part of the ceremony. Any chef worth his salt knows that the longer he keeps you waiting for his *pièce de résistance*, the hungrier you get and the more marvellous it will taste.

I proceeded to describe my own wedding day and how, because of my nervousness, I could hardly recall a single moment of what should have been the most memorable day of my life. She was worried that everyone would be staring at her.

I pointed out that this was the sole object of a wedding. That the bride is by far the most important person and that the groom is merely some pathetic acned object who, if he is lucky, rates a poor fourth behind the bridesmaids and the cake.

I also pointed out that this doesn't bother the groom in the slightest. He is just as nervous and is happy that the bride is the centre of attention. All that is important to him is to prove to his mates that he has captured the heart of the most beautiful girl in the world.

Now, on this occasion it happened to be true. I've had two brides and two daughters of my own, and I would hate for any of them to think that I was being disloyal. But isn't it a wonderful aspect of nature that any pregnant woman appears to be so attractive and healthy and that the bride is always far and away the most beautiful girl at a wedding.

By any standards Cheryl Stokes was and is an exceedingly beautiful girl. For those who are acquainted with the Stokes family, this might be something of a mystery. If Ronnie Stokes had been on the scene when they auditioned for *The Hunchback of Notre Dame*, Charles Laughton wouldn't have stood a chance.

Fortunately Cheryl resembles her mother Jean and on her wedding day she looked like a veritable princess. I pointed out to Cheryl that she looked like Elizabeth Taylor in her prime and that she had the choice of embarrassing herself and every other person attending that wedding by continuing to be embarrassed and shy and make the most important, and what should be the happiest, day of her life a nightmare, or she could walk down that aisle like the queen that she was, and make it a day that we could all look back on with happy memories, and most of all herself.

I was proud of Cheryl in that she blossomed from a child into a mature woman that day, not only at the wedding ceremony itself but at the reception. I would like to take credit for the transformation. However, if I'm honest, I've attended several other weddings during which the embarrassed and closed bud of an English rose has blossomed into full bloom without any lectures from me.

Just as the thousands of Cheryls over the ages have responded to the challenge, so you are going to respond to the challenge of achieving your goal. It might be that as you sit there like a queen or a king on that next flight, you will be with a partner, relative or friend who knows what you have achieved and is there to share in your triumph. If so, so much the better. But even if you stand on that rostrum alone, you will experience the exhilaration of achieving your goal unaided and your victory will be just as sweet.

Don't worry if between now and your flight you feel somewhat nervous and have butterflies in your stomach. This is all part of the exhilaration. Just think of hockey players when they come out for the final game of the Stanley Cup. They have the jitters, but at the same time they feel exhilarated. They have the jitters for exactly the same reason that you do: it's a big occasion in their lives and they want to perform well. You, however, hold a big advantage over them: only one team can win, but if you follow all of the instructions:

NO FORCE ON EARTH CAN PREVENT YOU FROM WINNING!

So, it's important to think positively and to maintain a happy frame of mind prior to the next flight. Now let's continue the comparison on:

THE DAY OF THE FLIGHT

23 The day of the flight

Whether it be a holiday or business trip, an air of excitement usually pervades the day of the flight. Even without a fear of flying, poor preparation can all too easily turn that pleasant feeling of excitement into bad temper and panic. So on the days prior to V (victory) day prepare a list of all the things you intend to take and a separate list of the absolute essentials:

* Air tickets and travel company's itinerary
* Passport
* Currency, traveller's cheques and credit card

If you have flown before you will already be familiar with the procedures I describe. It's not that I'm trying to teach my grandmother to suck eggs, but merely that I ask you to bear with those about to take their first flight, when lack of familiarity with the procedure can be disconcerting. I cannot emphasize strongly enough, whether the next flight be your first or thirtieth, the importance of remaining calm and serene and of avoiding anything that might disturb your equanimity.

It is usual for the travel agent to send an itinerary with the air tickets, giving details of both outward and return flights, including the airport, the name of the airline, the flight number, the time of the flight and the check-in time. This varies but is usually between 1 and 2 hours prior to the departure time. If the airport has more than one terminal the itinerary will also give the terminal number.

It is advisable to keep the air tickets, the itinerary and the passports in a separate wallet so that you have quick access to them at all times. It is rather inconvenient to have to open your suitcases once you've locked them and once you've checked-in you won't have access anyway. So pack a separate hold-all with anything you feel you might need prior to arriving at your hotel. You will have access to this hand-luggage during the journey.

I make no attempt to advise you what to include in your hand-luggage because this has been the cause of contention between Joyce and me in the past and the main object of this section is to avoid contention or aggravation in any form. Being a practical and logical male, I tend to concentrate on absolute essentials like a pack of cards, whereas Joyce tends to include more frivolous items such as a change of socks, toothbrush and face cloth. Being a democratic couple that has learned to give and take, we have a polite discussion and then include exactly what Joyce suggested in the first place. However, you should bear in mind that you might be travelling from wintry to summer conditions or vice versa.

I strongly recommend that you plan to arrive at the airport at least an hour before your check-in time. If you are thinking, "The last thing I want to do is spend an extra hour in that hell-hole", you've missed the point. By the time you've finished this book and you've finished the mental preparations, you won't see it as a hell-hole. Remember, this is your big day; by the end of it you'll be standing on that rostrum. You might have butterflies but you are going to enjoy your triumph. Start enjoying it now!

If you allow for that extra hour, you avoid the panic that can be caused by traffic jams or any other unforeseen delays. In any event there are distinct advantages in arriving early. You have plenty of time to park your car, to obtain a trolley for your luggage and to check the Visual Display Units (VDUs) which will tell you the number of your check-in counter. What's more, you won't have a long queue at the check-in counter and you'll have first choice of seats.

Which seats are the safest? I apologize, I'm just testing you. You need no more worry about which seats are the safest than you need worry about in which part of your garden it is safest to sit in case an aircraft crashes into it. Keep it clear in your mind. All the seats are safe and you are going to arrive safely. Do not torture yourself with negative and idiotic thoughts.

I would suggest that there is only one important consideration on your next flight: if you are worried about a fear of heights or feeling closed-in ask for an aisle seat, preferably situated level to the centre of the wings. This way you'll only be able to see the ground if you make a concentrated effort to do so. The disadvantage of an aisle seat is that you might miss the sometimes spectacular views afforded by a window seat.

At the check-in counter, you will be asked to produce your ticket and your passport and you will be given a boarding pass on which will be recorded your seat number. Keep the boarding pass in the same wallet as your ticket and passport. Your cases will be left at the check-in counter. The clerk will also advise you of the gate from which your aircraft will depart and the expected boarding time, which is usually between one half and three quarters of an hour prior to departure time.

The check-in area is surrounded by restaurants, bars, shops, washrooms, etc. However, no matter how much time you have available, I would recommend that you pass straight through to the departure lounge. Before you are allowed to enter, both you and your hand luggage will be screened. Screening is a perfectly painless process unless you happen to be carrying a gun or a bomb, which I do not recommend. You will also be required to produce your passport and boarding pass.

The departure lounge is also equipped with comfortable seating areas, bars, restaurants, washrooms and shops, including duty-free shops at which you can buy perfumes, cigarettes, alcoholic drinks, etc. at bargain prices. It is also equipped with a number of VDUs which provide you with up-to-date information about your flight, including any delays.

I wasn't so much concerned by the inconvenience of the delay on my first flight, but by the reason for it. Any regular customer will tell you that civil airlines are notoriously negligent about informing their clients about the length of and reason for delays. The little information that they do give you, far from relaxing you, tends to have the complete opposite effect:

"The delay is due to mechanical failure."

Oh my God! I'm going to be trapped inside some relic from WW2 that should have been scrapped 40 years ago. Or:

"The delay is due to the prevailing conditions at the destination airport."

Oh no! That must mean it's fog-bound or ice-bound. Our panic blocks our minds to the fact that our destination is Malaga airport in the middle of July and that no way can it be either fog-bound or ice-bound.

Remember, if there is a delay, no matter what the reason, there is no cause for alarm. In all probability the actual cause of the delay is to ensure your safety. Usually, the prevailing conditions at the airport of destination are because of a congestion of aircraft due to land about the same time. At one time the practice was to accumulate the aircraft waiting to land. Each one queuing up, circling the airport, waiting its turn to land. But here is an example of one of the safety features which has now been incorporated. The situation is anticipated, and rather than have the delay at 35,000 ft, circling the destination airport, the delay is transferred to the lounge of the airport of departure. Which way would you prefer to have it?

Occasionally circumstances require that the departing plane sits on the runway for an hour or so prior to take-off. This can be infuriating and inconvenient but before you get in a tizzy, ask yourself which is most important to you: to arrive on time or to arrive safely?

During the period of my terror of flying the inconvenience of the delay didn't bother me, but merely convinced me that flying was dangerous. In a way I suppose I actually enjoyed the delay. It postponed the terror and left me with an outside hope that the flight would be delayed indefinitely.

During the period that I was apprehensive about flying, a delay had the complete reverse effect: it confirmed that flying was safe, but annoyed me because it prolonged my apprehension. What is my attitude today? I'm philosophical. I accept that if you are flying to a holiday destination, the first day is spent in getting there. Even if I have to get up in the middle of the night in order to catch the flight and feel very tired it doesn't worry me. On the contrary, I'm elated! I'm on holiday! I can doze at the airport, during the flight and can lie in the next morning for as long as I want to.

Does it matter that you arrive at the airport an hour earlier, even if the flight is delayed for two hours? You are still living and it must be better than working. The longer the delay, the longer Joyce can indulge in her favourite pastime: spending my hard-earned money or, as she likes to call it, shopping! I pretend that it upsets me. But little does she know that all she is really doing is allowing me to luxuriate in my favourite pastime: reading!

Whether it be in the departure lounge or during the actual flight I can catch up on all those books that I promised myself one day I'd find the time to read. Airports are fascinating and wonderful places, provided your perspective is not distorted by an illogical fear of flying!

Several participants of the big Q confessed that they had tried to obliterate their FOF with alcohol. I confess that I'd tried the same tactic. Of course, if it worked, there would be no such thing as fear of flying, or any other fear for that matter. It seemed that we had all arrived at the same conclusion: no matter how much you drank, when you got on the plane you were stone-cold sober.

It would seem that other so-called relaxants, such as Valium, had no greater success in relieving the problem. This is not surprising. Really we know in our heart of hearts that the only cure for a problem is to remove the cause of the problem. One of the symptoms of the fear of flying is to feel physically tense. Not only do alcohol or Valium not remove the fear, they don't even remove the symptoms of the fear, but merely obliterate the symptoms of the fear from our minds. Once you have removed the fear, you won't need alcohol, Valium or any other illusory crutches.

Some airports have ceased the practice of announcing when each flight is about to board, together with last calls. So check occasionally with a VDU, and when your flight is ready for boarding, calmly make your way to the boarding gate. There is no need to rush; more than ample time is allowed for, and although the washrooms on the aircraft are perfectly adequate, they tend to be somewhat cramped and are often occupied, so it is advisable to take advantage of one of the washrooms in the departure lounge before boarding.

At the boarding gate there is a smaller lounge where the passengers for your particular flight are gathered prior to boarding. When actual boarding is announced you pass through the boarding gate and present your boarding pass. There is usually an enclosed walkway leading directly from the airport building into the aircraft.

The very worst aspect of flying is that there will be some Eugines on the plane. They invariably occupy the first five rows, get on the aircraft first and block the gangways while they stow their hand-luggage in the cupboards situated above their seats, causing a pile-up and general mayhem.

The sensible airlines announce boarding for the rear seats first, then the centre and front seats last. It would be even more sensible if the passengers were arranged in the departure lounge in their exact sequence, to avoid this problem. Some experts advise that you don't board the plane until the last possible moment so as to lessen the duration of the flight. Such a procedure merely serves to create panic rather than help to avoid it. This is your big day, you may have butterflies in your stomach but you are going to be serene and calm. In fact I would recommend that, when you arrive at the boarding gate, you inform the clerk that you are a nervous flyer and that you would like to be first on the plane. The staff are very sympathetic to nervous fliers and will go out of their way to accommodate you. You'll also find that you'll get VIP treatment throughout the flight. Best of all, when they see you cope majestically in spite of your declared nervousness, their respect will be apparent.

Far better to be first onto a spacious, empty plane, to have plenty of time to stow your hand-luggage, to put on your seat-belt, generally to acclimatize yourself and then sit back, relax and watch the Eugines creating chaos. If when you reach your seat the person behind you wishes to pass, let them do so before you stow your luggage. Also remember first to remove your book or any other object you might need during the flight.

If you arrive last on the plane, all the other passengers will be staring at you, they won't say a word but their expressions will clearly indicate that the plane would have taken off 10 minutes earlier had it not been for you.

Fear of flying can be very similar to shyness. If you are the last to arrive at the party, you form the impression that everyone else knows each other and is having a fantastic time. However, if you are the first to arrive, you can watch the later guests arrive, see how embarrassed and lost they appear to be, take the initiative, introduce yourself and so completely forget about your own shyness.

It's exactly the same on a flight: you can sit back calm and relaxed, studying the other passengers as they arrive, realizing that many of them are going through exactly the same trauma as you used to.

When all the passengers and crew are safely on board, the doors are closed and the aircraft will slowly taxi to the runway. During this time you will be shown the safety procedures. I have already described how, on my first flight, the process only served to increase my fear – obviously they were expecting some disaster to happen. Today I don't even bother to listen to the safety drill. Is that because I've flown so much that I already know it? No, it's because I know the odds against me ever having to use it are so remote as not to be worth bothering about.

If that's the case, why do they bother going through that procedure? Because they have to by law and because that attention to detail is why modern civil aviation is so safe. Do I not feel guilty in admitting that I don't even bother to listen to the safety procedures? No I don't! That is my privilege because I know I won't be needing them. Do you check where the fire extinguishers or fire exits are whenever you enter a cinema, theatre, store, hotel or public building? If not, you are being many times more irresponsible than I am. The only guilt I feel is that no one else seems to be taking any notice either yet the poor person still has to go through the routine.

Now we get to the whole crux of the matter. The real difference between why I was once so terrified of flying and now love to fly:

THE TAKE-OFF

24 The take-off

Like the idiots that spend much of their lives trying to move an object without actually touching it, purely with the power of thought, I would physically be trying to lift that plane off the runway. I was not only trying to do the pilot's job, but actually trying to assist the engines! I'd not been trained to fly myself and I knew nothing about aeronautics. Why was I trying to fly the plane?

Many experts give detailed information about the mechanics. Some information is essential. For example: on my first flight, no sooner had we taken off than the plane suddenly leaned over to the left. From an inside seat I suddenly found myself staring at the ground. I was convinced that something had gone wrong; either we had stalled, or that some mechanical fault had developed and that we were out of control and would soon come hurtling back to the ground, or that we were desperately trying to avoid a collision with another aircraft.

Now, I wasn't naive enough to believe that modern civil-airline pilots indulged in aerobatics. But no one had explained to me that aeroplanes turn in exactly the same way as bicycles and motor-cycles do and that it is perfectly natural. Try turning on a bicycle whilst remaining completely upright and you'll know what I mean. Perhaps it should have been obvious to me. But it wasn't.

Perhaps it should have been equally obvious that it would have been too much of a coincidence for the runway to have been pointing in the exact direction that we wished to travel and that once take-off had been completed, it would be natural to turn and consequently bank onto our correct course.

I like to think of myself as a reasonably intelligent person. But fear and intelligence are not ideal companions. I've no doubt that my basic fear of flying blocked out what should have been obvious to me. However, if only I had been prepared, at least that banked turn would not have increased my fear.

I believe the grunts and groans of the hydraulics caused me the most aggravation. I remember hearing the hydraulics almost immediately after the take-off and thinking: that's the undercarriage coming up, but isn't it a bit premature? Of course when the plane started to bank I was proved to be right – or thought I was. Can you see the point I'm making? Without any knowledge whatsoever, I was actually trying to fly the plane. Thinking I knew better than the pilot. Little wonder I was terrified.

It was even worse when we landed. Having successfully kept the plane in the air for over 2 hours, in spite of the deficiencies of the pilot and navigator, now all I have to do is land safely. It's obvious to me that he hasn't yet lowered the undercarriage and that he's leaving it a bit late. No doubt he's so intent on chatting up one of those beautiful hostesses that he's forgotten all about it.

Then bliss, sweet bliss. I can hear the grunts and groans announcing the lowering of the undercarriage. I sit back with a sigh of relief – another crisis averted. Suddenly the groans start again. Obviously the clumsy oaf has inadvertently hit the undercarriage button with his elbow and has actually retracted it. Or is it that the undercarriage is jammed or won't lock properly? I must have seen a hundred films where the undercarriage won't come down, or even worse, where the wheel will only come down beneath one wing. It didn't occur to me that we weren't flying a Spitfire.

There were two other major causes of panic on that first flight. The ping of the public-announcement system. A stewardess would go tearing down the aisle with a worried frown on her brow. Obviously something is desperately wrong. Her worried frown is because the captain has just asked for more coffee. At that exact moment a Eugine has been playing with his seat controls and has hit the button that demands attention from a stewardess. The poor girl has already had a bellyful of Eugine – you get one on every flight. Her instinct tells her to satisfy the captain's needs but company policy dictates that the customer comes first, and that is the reason for her worried frown.

The other major cause of panic was the regular change of the pitch in the sound of the engines. OK, I expected the initial thrust, but why was it that the sound died off so soon after take-off? No wonder I thought we had stalled or that there was some mechanical problem. And why after touching-down safely, when I thought the engines would be switched off, did they suddenly sound much louder?

This is reverse thrust. The pilot is actually using the engines as a brake. Don't worry, he doesn't have to, the aircraft is already equipped with an efficient and adequate braking system. Reverse thrust just makes it more efficient and more economical.

The point is that the pitch of the engines will change throughout the flight – that's normal. The PA system will chime throughout the flight – that's normal. If you are sitting there trying to assess every change in the sound of the engine, worrying about every chime, every turn, every groan on the hydraulics, you are trying to fly the plane! And because you are not qualified to fly it and cannot see what is actually happening, you are merely torturing yourself for no logical reason:

SO DON'T DO IT!!

This is your ninth and last instruction:

DON'T TRY TO FLY THE PLANE!

Do you think that people who spend a fortune on a luxury ocean cruise sit there trying to steer the ship, or wondering whether it will sink, or whether the captain and crew know their jobs? Of course they don't. They are there to enjoy themselves and that is exactly what they do.

You are in exactly the same position. You are not being driven by a Eugine and if you are worried that you are not in control, you are completely wrong. You have placed your confidence in the greatest experts in the world; do you feel you'd be in control if you were flying the plane?

So just accept that at various times throughout the flight the plane will turn and bank, the engines will raise or lower their pitch, you'll hear the grunts and groans of the hydraulics, the chimes will go and you might be asked to fasten your seat-belt in the middle of the flight. That doesn't mean that you are about to crash-land but that the captain is expecting turbulence. Remember severe turbulence is very rare and on the rare occasions you might experience it:

THERE IS NO DANGER!

The real difference between my first flight and my last is exactly that. On my first flight I was scared and, instead of having faith in the safety of civil aviation and the crew, my fear led me to doubt both and turned what should have been a pleasant and exhilarating experience into a nightmare. Because I know that flying itself is safe and that my life is in the hands of dedicated and incredibly skilled and competent people, even if I hear the grunt of the hydraulics, I don't even try to speculate whether it's the undercarriage going up or the slats moving. If I did I'd be trying to fly the plane. It would be like being driven by Eugine. So I'm quite happy to let the crew get on with their job – flying the plane – while they help me to get on with mine:

ENJOYING THE FLIGHT!

25   Enjoying the flight

At London Heathrow after the plane had safely landed they would announce over the PA system:

YOU ARE NOW ENTERING THE MOST DANGEROUS PART OF
YOUR JOURNEY

They were referring of course to the car ride from Heathrow to the centre of London. Statistically I knew that they were correct. But for some reason the import of the message never got through to me. My hands were still sweating from the ordeal of enabling the plane to land safely and my feeling of relief was so great that I couldn't wait to get into my car and drive home.

I realize now that part of the paradox was explained by the terminology. Just as if you ask: what is the most dangerous part of a flight, the take-off or landing? The question implies that there *is* danger. If they had rephrased the statement: you are now entering the least safe part of your journey, it might have had the desired effect, but by telling their passengers that driving is more dangerous than flying, they were merely confirming my fears that flying itself was dangerous.

Nowadays, I not only believe that driving is less safe than flying, but I'm very conscious and somewhat circumspect about the drive home, even when I'm the driver. I should point out that I am a very confident driver and, at the risk of appearing to be immodest, I believe that I am a very good driver. I'm not saying that I've transferred my fear of flying to a fear of driving. My interpretation of a very good driver is a very safe driver. I try to apply the same principles to my driving as the civil-aviation industry does to flying: SAFETY FIRST. For that reason, I do not fear driving, but I'm more conscious of the dangers than I used to be.

From the information obtained from the big Q, hours of discussion with sufferers from FOF and my own experiences, particularly the experience with Eugine, it became apparent that the difference between enjoying a journey and it being a nightmare depended purely on whether you felt safe.

Now, I'm aware that there are many reasons that a journey can be unpleasant even if you feel safe. For example: funeral processions travel at a speed that wouldn't cause palpitations to the most fearful traveller. Have you ever heard a single mourner say: "Oh we had the most wonderful journey to the cemetery!" So, if the reason for taking the journey is unpleasant, like a visit to the dentist, or a business trip that you wish you didn't have to take, it is not likely that you will enjoy the journey, no matter what your means of travel. However, the return journey can be exceedingly pleasant. You only have to stand outside a dentist's to observe the incredible change in the expression on the faces of patients when they walk out compared to when they walked in.

Another factor that can ruin an otherwise pleasant journey is the level of comfort. I'm terrified of fairground rides. If I bothered to research them I have absolutely no doubt I'd find that statistically they are safer than driving. I've no desire to do so, because even if they were as safe as elevators or flying, I get no pleasure from my stomach continuing to hurtle down in one direction when the rest of me has done a right turn.

The point I'm making is that there are several factors that can make a journey unpleasant which have little to do with safety. No matter how pleasant the journey might be, you won't enjoy it if it's a visit to the dentist. However, the reverse isn't true; if the reason for your journey is something very pleasant, you won't necessarily enjoy the journey. In fact the reason that you are reading this book is because a pleasant journey for a pleasant reason can be ruined by a fear of flying.

What I want to do is compare a car ride with a flight, having removed these extraneous factors. The reason for the journey is 2 weeks on the Costa del Sol. You have a modern comfortable car that has just been serviced and you aren't being driven by a Eugine, you are driving yourself. What could be better?

There were two major fears that were apparent from the big Q, and I found it difficult to assess which was the most important. I eventually came to the conclusion that it was the combination of these two fears that caused the fear of flying. The first we have already dealt with at length: the fear of mechanical breakdown. The second is:

I'M NOT IN CONTROL!

What makes you think that you are in control when you are driving your car? I agree that, providing your own car doesn't develop a fault, you are in control of it. You might not be a Eugine but you are literally surrounded by them. All hurtling along within a few feet of each other, cutting each other up, including you. How do you control them? Even if you are on a highway with a median, how do you prevent the Eugines on the other side from causing a pile-up, then catapulting over to your side and causing another pile-up there? It literally happens on the tiny island of Britain at least once every day. Do you know how many fatal accidents have occurred within the UK to flights within "THE LIMITATIONS" since 1990?

JUST THREE!!!

Do you know how many fatalities there were as a result of those accidents?

JUST FIFTEEN!!!

Just think of that. Only fifteen people in the UK have died in the last 8 years as a result of flying accidents within "THE LIMITATIONS". That's less than two people a year!

"But you're at 35,000 ft and I'm safely on terra firma!"

What's so safe about terra firma? When you next hurtle down the highway, trying to avoid the Eugines, just remember: I'm cocooned in my own private motorway. EUGINES aren't allowed up here. There aren't any obstacles at 35,000 ft, whether it be the hundreds of other cars or other objects that you can collide with on a road, always assuming that you don't doze off and leave the road.

"That may be true. But at least I'm driving. I'm in control!"

Bully for you. I don't wish to offend you, but my driver is far more skilled and competent than either you or me and you've already forgotten about all those other Eugines. Remember, the German Eugines drive at 150 mph.

"But at 35,000 ft supposing the engine stops or your pilot has a heart attack?"

No problem, I've got at least one spare engine and two spare pilots who can take over in an instant and are both just as capable as the captain. What happens to your passengers if you have a heart attack?

"But you are travelling at 500 mph and I'm only travelling at 70 mph. Surely 500 mph must be far more dangerous?"

It would be if I were travelling on the ground like you, surrounded by Eugines and other solid objects that would kill me if I hit them. But at 35,000 ft, there is nothing to hit. Remember, the earth travels at nearly 70,000 mph and in 3 billion years, it's never had a single accident. For a multitude of reasons, you are much safer at 35,000 ft than at ground level. Just think, what possible harm can you come to at 35,000 ft?

> "I take your point, but to get to 35,000 ft, that plane has to take off. And eventually it has to come down!"

Now you are beginning to see my point. At 35,000 ft it is completely safe. It is travelling at a speed that on the ground is really dangerous. It is only when taking off and landing that there is some risk. Even then the risk is so infinitesimal as to be not worth worrying about. The plane's speed will be far less than the average Formula 1 car travels at on a racing track. Even that speed will only be for a few seconds before it takes off and for seconds after it touches down. Even then, the track will be four times wider than the average racing track. It will be perfectly straight and there will be no other cars on the track. In the entire history of motor racing, which we regard as a risky sport, there is not one recorded fatality when those conditions have applied.

You should also bear in mind that those conditions will apply for less than 2 minutes. The entire flight to Spain is just over 2 hours. The drive is 2 days! Do you really want to waste 4 days of your holiday being pestered by the Eugines of this world when you can travel on cloud nine during the entire journey? We are nearly there now. All that remains is:

THE CONCLUSION

26 The conclusion

Fear is a friend. All fear is rational. As with the silver-back gorilla and the mirror, whilst he believed that his reflection was a rival, his fear was perfectly rational. His fear was based on a misconception. Once he understood that there was no reason for the fear, the fear was removed. However, had he retained the fear, then that fear would have been irrational.

BUT HE DIDN'T RETAIN THE FEAR!!!

A fear of flying is perfectly rational. It is also based on misconceptions. Once we have removed all those misconceptions, we will have removed the fear of flying. Unfortunately FOF is not as simple as the gorilla's problem. He had just one misconception to remove, whereas FOF is far more confused. Fear of flying is in fact a combination of several fears each caused by an even greater number of misconceptions.

Let us consider them again: flying is unnatural, heights, claustrophobia, suffocation, feeling trapped, bad weather, running out of fuel, crashes and collisions, mechanical failure, not being in control, sabotage, human error, traffic control, fire, falling from the sky.

Amazingly, not one participant in the big Q had a fear of train journeys. Are train journeys natural? They are no more natural than flying. Perhaps passenger travel by train appears to be more natural to us than flying because it was already a safe and accepted mode of transport when we were born, whereas the older ones of us have actually witnessed the evolution of safe civil aviation.

Trains are no less claustrophobic than airplanes and you won't suffocate in either. The risk of fire is just as great and, because trains travel at the same height along the same track, the risk of collision is even greater. You can't just get off a train when you want to any more than you can get off a plane. Trains are also subject to human failure, whether it be the signalman or the driver, and are just as prone to the weather or mechanical failure, as every regular train commuter knows. Because any fault in or object placed on the thousands of miles of track can cause derailment, trains are far more prone to sabotage than civil aircraft.

One of the major factors that sufferers of FOF complain of, is not being in control. How are you more in control on a train than you are on a plane? The point I'm making is that you don't need to feel in control of a train because you feel safe and secure. You won't need to feel in control of a plane once you feel safe and secure.

We're trying to remove the confusion; these other factors are merely red herrings. If they were the real cause of your fear of flying, you would also have a fear of train journeys.

So, having discounted the red herrings, what are we left with? What are the fears about plane journeys that don't apply to train journeys? There is no fear of heights on train journeys – if you do run out of fuel or have mechanical failure, you don't come crashing to the ground. As I have already explained, it is impossible to run out of fuel on a flight within "THE LIMITATIONS". The chances of two engines failing at the same time are over a billion to one against and, even if one of those probabilities were to happen, the plane will still fly, it doesn't drop like a stone to the ground.

Now, there is one further point that might disturb you. Smokers who attend our clinics find it difficult to believe that they can leave 4 hours later, already happy non-smokers and can remain so the rest of their lives. Many believe they have to go through a transitional period of trauma during which they have to continue to crave cigarettes.

Similarly, many alcoholics believe that, once they abstain, they have to go through a similar period of recovery and can never be cured completely. It illustrates the incredible power of the brainwashing that Western society subjects us to from birth. They can see so clearly that alcohol is the cause of their problem. What they seem completely blind to is that their lives were complete before they started taking alcohol and that they solve their problem the moment they stop taking it. For some reason they feel that they have to spend the rest of their lives bemoaning the fact that they can no longer subject themselves to the misery of being an alcoholic. Even more ludicrous, whilst they are consuming two bottles of whisky a day, they refuse to accept that they are alcoholics. But once they take the pledge, no alcohol might have touched their lips for 20 years, but they now describe themselves as alcoholics!

It's exactly the same with my weight-reduction method, "EASYWEIGH": you don't have to wait until you have reached the weight you wish to be. Like any problem in life, once you *know* that you have the solution, the problem is already solved. It's only if you doubt the solution that you have to wait for the proof of the pudding to become the eating. You might be thinking:

> "I can't contradict anything that you have said, but I still have a fear of flying. Must I wait for the proof of the pudding to become the eating when I take that next flight?"

No, that flight will take off and land safely, just as they always do. I took dozens of flights that took off and landed safely, but that didn't cure my fear of flying. I didn't need to fly to obtain a fear of flying, I had it before my first flight. The subsequent flights took off and landed safely, but they did nothing to remove my belief that flying was unnatural and dangerous.

A fear of flying is a purely mental problem based on misconceptions. Those misconceptions aren't removed because you risk your life a thousand times and are lucky enough to survive. They are only removed by realizing that they are misconceptions. You don't have to experience a safe flight in order to cure your fear of flying. Just as Adelle had already lost hers after our chat, and I lost mine during the research for this book, so it is essential that you have lost yours before you finish reading this book.

A fear of flying is rational if you have the misconceptions. By now we should have removed those misconceptions, and if you still have a fear of flying, it is not your fear that is irrational, but you. Unfortunately there are a few irrational people in this world. They have been blessed with the marvellous gift of life. All too often they are people who would appear to have no problems in life. They are attractive, healthy, wealthy and have nice families and friends. Yet for some strange reason they always seem to make life difficult for themselves, always seem to be swimming against the tide.

If you still have a fear of flying, it might be that you are one of those people; if so, you need to stop banging your head against the wall. Otherwise it might be that something hasn't registered. If so, try to analyse for yourself which misconception you have failed to remove. Go through Appendix B and ask yourself if you have religiously followed each instruction. If this doesn't solve the problem, re-read the text and if you still have a problem feel free to write to me.

The beautiful truth is that flying is incredibly safe, even during the time when we fear it. If you have opened your mind and followed all the instructions, you should now have the same feeling of excitement that Adelle and I had, straining like a dog at the leash to take that next flight. The choice is yours. The world is your oyster:

ENJOY OPENING THAT OYSTER
THERE'S A BEAUTIFUL PEARL INSIDE

APPENDIX A: Questionnaire

With a subject like fear of flying (FOF) it can be difficult to be objective. All I request is that you answer each question as honestly as you can. In attempting to do so, it may help you to know that this questionnaire will be read only by Allen Carr, a previously afflicted sufferer, and will be treated in strict confidence. Thank you.

Surname: First name:
Address:

Tel No: Age:

Does your FOF make you feel:	YES	NO
Ashamed?	11%	89%
Cowardly?	22%	78%
Irrational?	56%	44%
Stupid?	33%	67%
Inferior to people who don't suffer from FOF?	44%	56%

Apart from your FOF do you normally suffer from:		
Panic attacks	11%	89%
Claustrophobia?	22%	78%
Fear of heights?	67%	33%
Fear of driving?	11%	89%
Fear of being driven by:		
some other drivers?	89%	11%
all other drivers?	22%	78%
Fear of other forms of transport, e.g.:		
trains?	0%	100%
boats?	44%	56%
elevators?	33%	67%
escalators?	11%	89%
fairground rides?	78%	22%

Do you regard your FOF as a phobia?	67%	33%

**Do you lie to your friends and/or relatives
in order to disguise your FOF?** 22% 78%

**Do you believe that your FOF would cease
if you knew in advance that the plane
would land safely?** 78% 22%

Please list any other phobias you have not included above.

Why do you have a fear of flying?

Please list any questions which you feel should have been asked which haven't been and overleaf give brief a history of your FOF, including: when it started; what you think is the cause of it. Has it stopped you from flying? If not, has it got better or worse? Have you sought help?

APPENDIX B: The instructions

ALLEN CARR'S CLINICS

ALLEN CARR UK
Website: http://www.qwerty.co.
uk/allencarr

LONDON
1c Amity Grove
Raynes Park
London SW20 0LQ
Tel. & Fax: 0208 944 7761
Therapist: John Dicey
E-mail: postmaster@
allencarr.demon.co.uk

BIRMINGHAM
415 Hagley Road West
Quinton
Birmingham B32 2AD
Tel. & Fax: 0121 423 1227
Therapist: Jason Vale
E-mail: JASEYBEAN@
AOL.COM

BRISTOL
Tel.: 0117 908 1106
Therapist: John Emery

DEVON
Angel Cottage

Cutteridge Farm
Whitestone
Exeter EX4 2HE
Tel.: 01392 811603
Therapist: Trevor Emdon
E-mail: trevor@emdon.
freeserve.co.uk

EDINBURGH
48 Eastfield
Joppa
Edinburgh EH15 2PN
Tel. & Fax: 0131 660 6688
Therapist: Derek McGuff
E-mail: easyway@
clara.co.uk

GLASGOW
Meadow House
Meadowmill
Tranent EH33 ILZ
Tel.: 01875 616658
Therapist: Joe Bergin

KENT
Tel.: 01227 779188
Therapist: Angela Jouanneau

NORTH EAST
10 Dale Terrace
Dalton-le-Dale
Seaham
County Durham SR7 8QP
Tel. & Fax: 0191 581 0449
Therapist: Tony Attrill

SOUTH COAST
Christchurch Business Centre
Grange Road
Christchurch
Dorset BH23 41D
Tel.: 01425 272757
Fax: 01425 274250
Therapist: Anne Emery
E-mail: AEmery3192@
aol.com

SOUTHAMPTON
Tel.: 01425 272757
Fax: 01425 274250
Therapist: Anne Emery
E-mail: AEmery3192@
aol.com

YORKSHIRE
Tel.: 0700 900 0305
Fax: 01904 340 159
Mobile: 07931 597 588
Therapist: Diana Evans
E-mail: DIANAYORK@
FSBDIAL.CO.UK

ALLEN CARR AUSTRALIA
MELBOURNE
148 Central Road
Nunawading
Vic 3131, Victoria
Tel. & Fax: 03 9894 8866
Therapist: Trudy Ward
E-mail: easywaya@
bigpond.com

SYDNEY
40 Ashbrookes Road
Mount White, NSW 2250
Tel.: 02 9328 2978
Therapist: John Ryff
E-mail:
John_Ryff@
compuware.com

ALLEN CARR AUSTRIA
Website: http://
www.allen-carr.at

VIENNA
Tel.: 01 333 1355
Fax: 08031 463068
Therapist: Erich Kellermann
E-mail: erich.
kellermann@allen-carr.at

SALZBURG
Tel.: 0662 878718
Fax: 08031 463068
Therapist: Erich Kellermann
E-mail: erich.
kellermann@allen-carr.at

ALLEN CARR BELGIUM

ANTWERP
Marialei 47
2018 Antwerpen
Tel.: 03 281 6255
Fax: 03 744 0608
Therapist: Dirk Nielandt
E-mail: easyway@
online.be

ALLEN CARR CANADA

TORONTO
461 North Service Road
Unit B7
Oakville
Ontario L6M 2V5
Tel.: 905 827 3888
Fax: 905 827 9434
Therapist: Nancy Toth
E-mail: aceasyway@
msn.com

ALLEN CARR ECUADOR

QUITO
Veintimilla 878 y Amazonas
PO Box 17-03-179
Quito
Tel. & Fax: 02 56 33 44
Tel.: 02 82 09 20
Therapist: Ingrid Wittich
E-mail: toisan@ECNET.ec

ALLEN CARR FRANCE
Website: http.//www.allencarr.fr
E-mail: info@allencarr.fr

MARSEILLE
70 Rue St Ferreol
13006 Marseille
Tel.: 04 91 33 54 55
Fax: 04 91 33 32 77
Therapist: Erick Serre
E-mail: info@allencarr.fr

ALPES
Centre Allen Carr ALPES
BP 203
73277 Albertville
Cedex
Tel.: 04 79 37 76 02
Fax: 04 79 32 84 72
Therapist: Daniel Gille
E-mail: easyalpes@minitel.net

ROUSSILLON
1 Rue Pierre Curie,
66000 Perpignan
Tel.: 04 68 34 40 68
Fax: 04 68 62 16 09
Therapist: Eugene Salas
E-mail: eugenesalas@
minitel.net

CARIBBEAN
11 Lot du Moulin
97190 Gosier

Guadeloupe
Antilles
Tel.: 05 90 84 95 21
Fax: 05 90 84 60 87
Therapist: Fabiana de Oliveira
E-mail: allencaraibes@
wandoo.fr

ALLEN CARR GERMANY
Website: http://
www.allen-carr.de
E-mail: info@allen-carr.de

MUNICH
Samweg 14
82281 Porgen
Tel.: 08134 559560
Fax: 08134 559561
Therapists: Petra Wackerle &
    Stephan Kraus
E-mail: info@allen-carr.de

STUTTGART
Heumadener Str. 11
70329 Stuttgart-Hedelfingen
Tel.: 0711 4209154
Fax: 08135 8920
Therapists: Petra Wackerle &
    Stephan Kraus
E-mail: info@allen-carr.de

BAD SULZUFLEN
Im neuen Land 20a
32107 Bad Salzuflen

Tel.: 05222 797622
Fax: 05222 797624
Therapist: Wolfgang Rinke
E-mail: wolfgang.rinke@
allen-carr.de

DÜSSELDORF
Steffenstr. 4
40545 DÅsseldorf
Tel.: 0211 5571738
Fax: 0211 5571740
Therapist: Axel Matheja
E-mail: axel.matheja@
allen-carr.de

BERLIN
Tel.: 030 21750488
Fax: 030 21750489
E-mail: info@allen-carr.de

HAMBURG
Tel.: 040 28051056
Therapist: Regina Hildebrandt
E-mail: regina.
hildebrandt@allen-carr.de

FRANKFURT
Tel.: 06701 960673
Therapist: Elfi Blume
E-mail: elfi.blume@
allen-carr.de

ALLEN CARR HOLLAND

AMSTERDAM
Pythagorasstraat 22
1098 GC Amsterdam
Tel.: 020 465 4665
Fax: 020 465 6682
Therapist: Eveline De Mooij
E-mail: allencarr@
mooy.demon.nl

UTRECHT
De Beaufortlaan 22 B
3768 MJ Soestduinen
(gem. Soest)
Tel. (stop smoking): 035 60 29458
Therapist: Paula Rooduijn
E-mail: paula@
rooduyn.demon.nl
Tel. (weight): 035 60 32153
Fax: 035 60 32265
Therapist: Nicolette de Boer
E-mail: nicolette@
allencarr.nl

ROTTERDAM
Mathenesserlaan 290
3021 HV Rotterdam
Tel.: 010 244 07 09
Fax: 010 244 07 10
Therapist: Kitty van't Hof
E-mail: carr.
rotterdam@wxs.nl

ALLEN CARR HONG KONG

WANCHAI
Suite B
19th Floor
Lo Yong Court Commercial
   Building
Wanchai
Tel.: 852 2893 1571
Fax: 852 2554 2958
Therapists: Jon Lewis-Evans &
   Leo Ngai
E-mail: easyway@
hkwww.com

ALLEN CARR ICELAND

REYKJAVIK
Ljosheimar 4
104 Reykjavik
Tel.: 354 553 9590
Fax: 354 588 7060
Therapists: Petur Einarsson &
   Valgeir Skagfjord
E-mail: pein@ismennt.is

ALLEN CARR IRELAND

DUBLIN
123 Coolamber Park
Templeogue
Dublin 16
Tel.: 01 494 1644
Tel. & Fax: 01 493 9313
Therapist: Brenda Sweeney
E-mail: seansw@iol.ie

ALLEN CARR ISRAEL

JERUSALEM
PO Box 127
Givat Ze'ev
Tel.: 02 624 2586
Therapist: Michael Goldman

ALLEN CARR ITALY

MILAN
Studio Pavanello
Piazza Argentina 4
20124 Milan
Mobile Tel.: 0348 354 7774 or
    0322 980 350
Therapist: Francesca Cesati

ALLEN CARR SOUTH
AFRICA

CAPETOWN
PO Box 5269
Helderberg
Somerset West 7135
Tel.: 083 600 5555
Fax: 083 8 600 5555
Therapist: Dr Charles Nel
E-mail: easyway@
allencarr.co.za

ALLEN CARR SPAIN

MADRID
C/Fernandez De Los Rios
106, 1. IZQ
28015 Madrid
Tel.: 91 543 8504
Therapists: Geoffrey Molloy &
    Rhea Sivi
E-mail: sivimoll@arrakis.es

ALLEN CARR SWITZERLAND
Website: http://www.
allen-carr.ch

ZURICH
Bernhofstr. 34
CH-8134 Adliswil
Tel.: 0041 1 7105678
Fax: 0041 1 7105683
Therapist: Cyrill Argast
E-mail: cyrill.argast@
allen-carr.ch

ALLEN CARR USA

TEXAS
12823 Kingsbridge Lane
Houston
Texas 77077
Tel.: 281 597 1904
Fax: 281 597 9829
Therapist: Laura Cattell
E-mail: ACatt38826@
aol.com

NEW JERSEY
Tel.: 732 730 1850 or
1 800 524 9949
Therapist: Keith Newmark
E-mail: acezway@juno.com

ST LOUIS
Tel.: 1 800 524 9949
Therapist: Keith Newmark
E-mail: acezway@juno.com